# Addressing Corruption Allegations in International Arbitration

# International Investment Law and Arbitration



Volumes published in this Brill Research Perspectives title are listed at *brill.com/rpia*

# Addressing Corruption Allegations in International Arbitration

*By*

Brody K. Greenwald and Jennifer A. Ivers

BRILL

LEIDEN | BOSTON

This paperback book edition is simultaneously published as Volume 2(3) 2018, in *International Investment Law and Arbitration*, DOI:10.1163/24055778-12340006.

Typeface for the Latin, Greek, and Cyrillic scripts: "Brill". See and download: brill.com/brill-typeface.

ISBN 978-90-04-36977-1 (paperback)
ISBN 978-90-04-41091-6 (e-book)



This book is printed on acid-free paper and produced in a sustainable manner.

# Contents

# Addressing Corruption Allegations in International Arbitration

*Brody K. Greenwald*
White & Case LLP
*bgreenwald@whitecase.com*

*Jennifer A. Ivers*
U.S. Department of Commerce
*jivers@doc.gov*

## Abstract

In *Addressing Corruption Allegations in International Arbitration*, Brody K. Greenwald and Jennifer A. Ivers provide a comprehensive overview of the key issues that arise in international arbitrations involving allegations of corruption drawing upon their significant experience in these high-stakes cases, including in the only two reported investment treaty cases dismissed specifically as a result of corruption. Their monograph is a valuable resource guide that analyzes, among other things, the public policy against corruption, the requirements for establishing corruption, issues relating to the burden and standard of proof, how corruption has been proved in practice, and the legal consequences where corruption is established. Mr. Greenwald and Ms. Ivers also assess issues that arise where a sovereign State raises an arbitration defense based on alleged corruption, but does not prosecute the alleged wrongdoers in its domestic courts.

## Keywords

international arbitration – corruption – bribery – proof – consequences

 | DOI:10.1163/9789004410916_002

## I Introduction

Allegations of corruption are now frequently raised in international arbitration. Tribunals have been called upon to resolve serious accusations of bribes allegedly paid to judges, high-level government officials, or their friends or relatives in order to rig tenders and secure necessary approvals or favorable court judgments. We have been on the front lines acting as counsel in many of these disputes, including in the only two reported investment treaty cases ever dismissed due to the tribunal finding that the investor made its investment through corruption.[1]

We discuss below the key issues that arise in cases where corruption is alleged and aim to make a small contribution to what rightly has been described as the "burgeoning scholarship on corruption in investment arbitration."[2] First, we demonstrate that although corruption is strongly condemned as contrary to international public policy, it remains endemic in much of the world.

Second, we discuss the requirements for establishing corruption. Specifically, we consider what must be proven to establish the crime of bribery of a foreign public official.

Third, we address issues concerning the burden and standard of proof. It is a well-settled principle of international law that the party raising an allegation has the legal burden of proving it. The party alleging corruption therefore must prove it occurred. As to the standard of proof, while most allegations must be shown to be more likely true than not true, allegations of corruption and fraud typically require a higher standard of proof or more compelling evidence. Corruption nevertheless may be proven through circumstantial evidence and adverse inferences.

Fourth, we explain how corruption has been proven in practice. In a few cases, parties have admitted the facts establishing that they bribed a foreign public official. In general, however, proving corruption is exceedingly difficult because bribes typically are concealed through complex (and seemingly legitimate) transactions with third parties.

Fifth, we consider the consequences in cases where corruption is established. There is no question that taking retaliatory State action against an

---

1 These two cases, *Metal-Tech v. Uzbekistan* and *Spentex v. Uzbekistan*, are discussed below. The views expressed in this monograph are those of the authors and do not necessarily reflect the views of White & Case LLP, its clients, or the Government of the United States of America. The authors wish to thank Jillian Casey, Claire-Naila Damamme, and Kanika Vaish for their assistance in preparing this monograph.

2 Aloysius Llamzon, "State Responsibility for Corruption: The Attribution Asymmetry in International Investment Arbitration," Transnational Dispute Management, Vol. 10, Issue 3 at 1.

investor and causing it damage for refusing to pay a bribe would violate a State's obligation to accord fair and equitable treatment, should such protections apply under the applicable investment treaty, law, or contract. It also is widely accepted that claims arising out of a contract or an investment made through corruption will be dismissed. By contrast, corruption or other illegality occurring after the investment was made generally will not give rise to a jurisdictional or admissibility defense, although it may have consequences for the merits of the claims or the amount of compensation awarded.

Finally, we consider whether the bribe itself should be attributed to the State and whether the State should be precluded from raising allegations of bribery in the arbitration if it does not prosecute the alleged corruption in its domestic courts.

## II Despite Longstanding Efforts to Combat Corruption, It Remains Endemic in Much of the World

A United Nations publication defines corruption in general terms as "the misuse of a public or private position for direct or indirect personal gain," and observes that "[a]ttempts to develop a more precise definition invariably encounter legal, criminological and, in many countries, political problems."[3] As commonly understood, corruption broadly encompasses crimes such as bribery, insider dealing, and influence-peddling, as well as abuse of power, nepotism, revolving doors between the private and public sectors, and conflicts of interest.[4]

The international community has adopted a number of measures to combat the bribery of public officials. In the wake of the Watergate political scandal in the United States, the U.S. Congress found that companies were engaged in "widespread global corruption" and were using secret slush funds to make illegal campaign contributions and also to pay bribes to foreign officials to secure business abroad.[5] Congress concluded that corruption was not merely a domestic issue, but "a global problem" that "undermines democratic values and public accountability," "weakens the rule of law," and "threatens stability

3 United Nations Handbook on Practical Anti-Corruption Measures for Prosecutors and Investigators (Sept. 2004) at 23.

4 *See, e.g.*, European Commission, Migration and Home Affairs, "Corruption," available at https://ec.europa.eu/home-affairs/what-we-do/policies/organized-crime-and-human-trafficking/corruption_en (last accessed Apr. 15, 2019).

5 A Resource Guide to the U.S. Foreign Corrupt Practices Act by the Criminal Division of the U.S. Department of Justice and the Enforcement Division of the U.S. Securities and Exchange Commission (2012) ("FCPA Resource Guide") at 2–3.

and security by facilitating criminal activity within and across borders, such as the illegal trafficking of people, weapons, and drugs."[6] The United States therefore enacted the first major legislation prohibiting the bribery of foreign public officials through the Foreign Corrupt Practices Act ("FCPA") of 1977.[7]

Two decades later, in Caracas, Venezuela, the member States of the Organization of American States enacted the first international convention to address corruption, the Inter-American Convention against Corruption of 1996, now ratified or acceded to by each member State except Cuba.[8] The State parties to the Convention expressed their conviction that "corruption undermines the legitimacy of public institutions and strikes at society, moral order and justice, as well as at the comprehensive development of peoples."[9] The State parties therefore agreed to adopt, to the extent that they had not already done so, measures to prohibit corruption, including transnational bribery, under their domestic laws and to cooperate among themselves in combating such corruption.[10]

Over the next several years, nearly every State across the globe ratified one or more similar international anticorruption conventions, including, among others, the Organisation for Economic Co-operation and Development ("OECD") Convention on Combating Bribery of Foreign Public Officials in International Business Transactions of 1997, ratified or acceded to by 44 States;[11] the European Union Convention against Corruption involving Officials of 1997, ratified or acceded to by each EU member State except the Czech Republic

6 *Id.* at 2–3 (further noting that corruption is "also bad for business" and "anti-competitive, leading to distorted prices and disadvantaging honest businesses that do not pay bribes. It increases the cost of doing business globally and inflates the cost of government contracts in developing countries."). *See also id.* Preamble (quoting the U.S. Senate's similar declaration in 1977).

7 The FCPA also prescribes civil and criminal penalties for knowingly falsifying books and records or circumventing or failing to implement an adequate system of internal accounting controls.

8 Inter-American Convention Against Corruption (B-58), adopted Mar. 29, 1996, entered into force Mar. 6, 1997. For ratification status, *see* http://www.oas.org/en/sla/dil/inter_american_treaties_B-58_against_Corruption_signatories.asp (last accessed Apr. 15, 2019).

9 Inter-American Convention Against Corruption (B-58), adopted Mar. 29, 1996, entered into force Mar. 6, 1997, Preamble.

10 *Id.* Arts. III, VII–VIII.

11 Organisation for Economic Co-operation and Development Convention on Combating Bribery of Foreign Public Officials in International Business Transactions, adopted Dec. 17, 1997, entered into force Feb. 15, 1999. For ratification status, *see* http://www.oecd.org/daf/anti-bribery/WGBRatificationStatus.pdf (last accessed Apr. 15, 2019).

and Malta;[12] the Council of Europe Criminal Law Convention on Corruption of 1999, ratified or acceded to by 48 States;[13] the Council of Europe Civil Law Convention on Corruption of 1999, ratified or acceded to by 35 States;[14] the United Nations Convention against Transnational Organized Crime of 2000, ratified or acceded to by 189 States as of July 2018;[15] the Economic Community of West African States Protocol on the Fight against Corruption of 2001, pending ratification;[16] the South African Development Community Protocol against Corruption of 2001, ratified by 13 States;[17] the African Union Convention on Preventing and Combating Corruption of 2003, ratified or acceded to by 40 States;[18] and the United Nations Convention against Corruption of 2003, the only legally binding universal anticorruption instrument now ratified or acceded to by 186 States.[19]

12 European Union Convention against Corruption involving Officials, adopted May 26, 1997, entered into force Sept. 28, 2005, available at https://eur-lex.europa.eu/legal-content/EN/TXT/?uri=LEGISSUM:l33027 (last accessed Apr. 15, 2019).

13 Council of Europe Criminal Law Convention on Corruption, ETS No. 173, opened for signature Jan. 27, 1999, entered into force July 1, 2002. For ratification status, *see* https://www.coe.int/en/web/conventions/full-list/-/conventions/treaty/173/signatures?p_auth=dDQSkcXJ (last accessed Apr. 15, 2019).

14 Council of Europe Civil Law Convention on Corruption, ETS No. 174, opened for signature Nov. 4, 1999, entered into force Nov. 1, 2003. For ratification status, *see* https://www.coe.int/en/web/conventions/full-list/-/conventions/treaty/174/signatures?p_auth=XJZVAsQx (last accessed Apr. 15, 2019).

15 United Nations Convention against Transnational Organized Crime and the Protocols Thereto, Resolution 55/25, adopted Nov. 15, 2000, entered into force Sept. 29, 2003. For ratification status, *see* https://treaties.un.org/pages/ViewDetails.aspx?src=TREATY&mtdsg_no=XVIII-12&chapter=18&clang=_en (last accessed Apr. 15, 2019).

16 Economic Community of West African States Protocol on the Fight against Corruption, opened for signature Dec. 21, 2001 (not yet in force), available at https://eos.cartercenter.org/uploads/document_file/path/406/ECOWAS_Protocol_on_Corruption.pdf (last accessed Apr. 15, 2019).

17 South African Development Community Protocol against Corruption, adopted Aug. 14, 2001, entered into force Aug. 6, 2003. For ratification status, *see* https://actsouthernafrica.wordpress.com/2017/05/17/status-on-the-signature-and-ratification-of-anti-corruption-instruments-by-sadc-member-states/ (last accessed Apr. 15, 2019).

18 African Union Convention on Preventing and Combating Corruption, adopted July 1, 2003, entered into force Aug. 5, 2006. For ratification status, *see* https://au.int/sites/default/files/treaties/36382-sl-african_union_convention_on_preventing_and_combating_corruption.pdf (last accessed Apr. 15, 2019).

19 United Nations Convention Against Corruption, Resolution 58/4, adopted Oct. 31, 2003 by the UN General Assembly, entered into force Dec. 14, 2005 ("U.N. Convention Against Corruption"). For ratification status, see https://www.unodc.org/unodc/en/corruption/ratification-status.html (last accessed Apr. 15, 2019).

In the foreword to the U.N. Convention against Corruption, the late Kofi Annan, then the Secretary-General of the United Nations, remarked that the Convention sent "a clear message" that the international community was "determined to prevent and control corruption" and that "betrayal of the public trust will no longer be tolerated."[20] He further declared:

> Corruption is an insidious plague that has a wide range of corrosive effects on societies. It undermines democracy and the rule of law, leads to violations of human rights, distorts markets, erodes the quality of life and allows organized crime, terrorism and other threats to human security to flourish.
>
> This evil phenomenon is found in all countries—big and small, rich and poor—but it is in the developing world that its effects are most destructive. Corruption hurts the poor disproportionately by diverting funds intended for development, undermining a Government's ability to provide basic services, feeding inequality and injustice and discouraging foreign aid and investment. Corruption is a key element in economic underperformance and a major obstacle to poverty alleviation and development.[21]

Against this backdrop, arbitral tribunals have recognized that corruption violates both domestic laws and international public policy. In an arbitration submitted to the International Centre for the Settlement of Investment Disputes ("ICSID"), the tribunal in *World Duty Free v. Kenya* found that "bribery or influence peddling, as well as both active and passive corruption, are sanctioned by criminal law in most, if not all, countries."[22] The *World Duty Free* tribunal further observed that, in concluding the conventions discussed above, "States have shown their common will to fight corruption, not only through national legislation, as they did before, but also through international cooperation. In doing so, States not only reached a new stage in the fight against corruption, but also solidly confirmed their prior condemnation of it."[23] The tribunal therefore concluded that "bribery is contrary to the international

---

20 *Id.* Foreword by U.N. Secretary-General Kofi Annan (stating that the Convention "will reaffirm the importance of core values such as honesty, respect for the rule of law, accountability and transparency in promoting development and making the world a better place for all").

21 *Id.* Foreword by U.N. Secretary-General Kofi Annan.

22 *World Duty Free Co. Ltd. v. The Republic of Kenya*, ICSID Case No. ARB/00/7, Award dated Oct. 4, 2006 ("*World Duty Free v. Kenya*") ¶ 142.

23 *Id.* ¶ 146.

public policy of most, if not all, States or, to use another formula, to transnational public policy."[24]

Many other international tribunals have made similar observations. Thus, for example:

- The ICSID tribunal in *Metal-Tech v. Uzbekistan* observed that "the condemnation of corruption" applicable under the laws of Uzbekistan in that case was "in conformity with international law and the laws of the vast majority of States."[25]
- The ICSID tribunal in *Churchill Mining v. Indonesia* endorsed the observations of the *World Duty Free* and *Metal-Tech* tribunals and commented that "particularly serious cases of fraudulent conduct, such as corruption, have been held to be contrary to international or transnational public policy."[26]
- The ICSID tribunal in *Niko v. Bangladesh* found wide acceptance for the view "that the prohibition of bribery is of such importance for the international legal order that it forms part of what has been described as international or transnational public policy."[27]
- The ICSID tribunal in *Kim v. Uzbekistan* remarked that corruption violates international public policy and "is antithetical to the rule of law in its broadest sense."[28]
- The tribunal in *Croatia v. MOL*, an arbitration administered by the Permanent Court of Arbitration ("PCA") under the United Nations Commission on International Trade Law ("UNCITRAL") arbitration rules, commented: "There can be no doubt as to the gravity of corruption in the

24 *Id.* ¶ 157.

25 *Metal-Tech Ltd. v. The Republic of Uzbekistan*, ICSID Case No. ARB/10/3, Award dated Oct. 4, 2013 ("*Metal-Tech v. Uzbekistan*") ¶ 290 (also finding that the international community of States had "sought to address the issue of corruption with a targeted effort to eliminate corrupt practices in the public service sector and criminal corruption in domestic legal orders"). *Id.* ¶ 290 (affirming the *World Duty Free* tribunal's finding that corruption is contrary to transnational public policy). White & Case LLP represented the Republic of Uzbekistan in this case.

26 *Churchill Mining PLC and Planet Mining Pty Ltd v. Republic of Indonesia*, ICSID Cases Nos. ARB/12/14 and ARB/12/40, Award dated Dec. 6, 2016 ¶ 493.

27 *Niko Resources (Bangladesh) Ltd. v. People's Republic of Bangladesh, Bangladesh Petroleum Exploration & Production Company Limited, and Bangladesh Oil Gas and Mineral Corporation*, ICSID Cases Nos. ARB/10/11 and ARB/10/18, Decision on Jurisdiction dated Aug. 19, 2013 ("*Niko v. Bangladesh*") ¶ 431; *id.* ¶¶ 432–433.

28 *Vladislav Kim and others v. Republic of Uzbekistan*, ICSID Case No. ARB/13/6, Decision on Jurisdiction dated Mar. 8, 2017 ("*Kim v. Uzbekistan*") ¶¶ 543, 593 (further observing that "[t]he international community, many nations and many investors have repeatedly stressed the importance of combatting corruption"). White & Case LLP represents the Republic of Uzbekistan in this case.

modern world.... It is thus generally accepted that corruption is a cancer that eats into the body politic."[29]

Regrettably, despite the substantial efforts of many States and international organizations to stamp out corruption, bribes are still routinely demanded and paid.[30] Thus, in a speech praising the "incredible degree" to which "states have now reached a consensus on the condemnation of the bribery of foreign officials by individuals and companies—what is also known as transnational corruption," Yves Fortier stated that as Chairman of the World Bank's Sanctions Board from 2012–2015, he "learned how fraud and corruption were rampant in projects financed by the World Bank."[31]

These observations are confirmed by quantitative analyses of corruption. From March 2014 to January 2017, the anticorruption organization Transparency International interviewed over 162,000 adults from 119 countries around the globe. Transparency International reported that nearly one in four people stated that they had paid a bribe within the past year, and that the results of its interviews were broadly consistent across many regions of the world.[32]

At a meeting of the U.N. Security Council held in September 2018, U.N. Secretary-General António Guterres commented on a similar finding by the World Bank that businesses and individuals pay more than US$ 1 trillion in bribes every year.[33] The Secretary-General warned the Security Council that the cost of these bribes on the global economy is staggering and, according to recent estimates of the World Economic Forum, is at least US$ 2.6 trillion per year—or 5% of the global gross domestic product.[34]

29 *The Republic of Croatia v. MOL Hungarian Oil and Gas PLC*, PCA Case No. 2014–15, UNCITRAL, Final Award dated Dec. 23, 2016 ("*Croatia v. MOL*") ¶¶ 92, 95.

30 *Id.* ¶ 95 (observing that corruption is still "endemic in certain parts of the world").

31 Alison Ross, "Fortier takes lead in development bank's corruption battle," Global Arbitration Review dated Sept. 20, 2016, available at https://globalarbitrationreview.com/article/1068603/fortier-takes-lead-in-development-bank%E2%80%99s-corruption-battle (last accessed Apr. 15, 2019).

32 Transparency International, Global Corruption Barometer dated Nov. 14, 2017 (reporting bribery rates of 20% in accession countries, 23% in sub-Saharan Africa, 28% in Asia Pacific, 29% in Latin America and the Caribbean, 30% in the Middle East and North Africa, and 30% in the Commonwealth of Independent States), available at https://www.transparency.org/news/feature/global_corruption_barometer_citizens_voices_from_around_the_world (last accessed Apr. 15, 2019).

33 U.N. Security Council 8346th Meeting, SC/13493 dated Sept. 10, 2018, "Global Cost of Corruption at Least 5 Per Cent of World Gross Domestic Product, Secretary-General Tells Security Council, Citing World Economic Forum Data," available at https://www.un.org/press/en/2018/sc13493.doc.htm (last accessed Apr. 25, 2019).

34 *Id.*

Notably, as the number of cases administered by ICSID has more than quadrupled in the past 15 years,[35] nearly 80% of those cases have been brought against States that rank in the bottom quarter of Transparency International's index of corruption perceptions.[36] In other words, the number of investor-State cases is continuing to increase, and the large majority of those cases concern investments in States that are considered especially corrupt. In all likelihood, allegations of corruption thus will continue to be a focal point of international investment disputes.

## III The Requirements for Establishing Corruption

The U.N. Convention against Corruption requires each of its 186 State parties to prohibit the bribery of their own national public officials, foreign public officials, and officials of public international organizations.[37] Article 16(1) of the Convention provides:

> Each State Party shall adopt such legislative and other measures as may be necessary to establish as a criminal offence, when committed intentionally, the promise, offering or giving to a foreign public official or an official of a public international organization, directly or indirectly, of an undue advantage, for the official himself or herself or another person or entity, in order that the official act or refrain from acting in the exercise of his or her official duties, in order to obtain or retain business or other undue advantage in relation to the conduct of international business.[38]

Arbitral tribunals considering similar definitions of corruption under various national laws have observed that three requirements must be established:

---

35 ICSID administered 63 cases in 2003 and 258 cases in 2017. Annual Report of the International Centre for the Settlement of Investment Disputes, Annual Report for 2017 at 30.

36 Transparency International, Corruption Perceptions Index 2017 dated Feb. 21, 2018, available at https://www.transparency.org/news/feature/corruption_perceptions_index_2017 (last accessed Apr. 15, 2019).

37 U.N. Convention Against Corruption Arts. 15(a), 16(1). The Convention further requires State Parties to prohibit the "solicitation or acceptance" of bribes by national public officials. *Id.* Art. 15(b). It does not, however, require State Parties to prohibit foreign public officials or officials of public international organizations from soliciting or accepting bribes, but instead merely directs State Parties to "consider" adopting such prohibitions. *Id.* Art. 16(2).

38 *Id.* Art. 16(1).

(i) the promise, offer, or giving of something of value; (ii) intended for a public official or another person or entity; (iii) in order for that official to take or refrain from taking official action.[39]

A few observations are worth noting. First, the bribe need not be cash or even property; it may be anything of value that confers an improper benefit.[40]

Second, a crime is committed upon the offer or promise to give a bribe, even if the bribe is not paid until much later in time or is never paid at all.[41]

Third, the bribe must be offered, promised, or given "in order to obtain or retain business or other undue advantage in relation to the conduct of international business." Typically in investor-State arbitrations, allegations of bribery relate to the government's approval of the investment and this requirement therefore *a fortiori* is satisfied. Bribes paid to gain a competitive advantage in the operation of a business also satisfy this so-called "business purpose test."[42]

Fourth, the person offering the bribe does not need to know the identity of the ultimate beneficiary. Authorizing a subordinate or a third party to pay whomever needs to be paid is unlawful even if no bribe is ultimately paid or even offered.[43]

Fifth, it is unlawful to offer or give a bribe to a foreign public official to take or refrain from taking official action even if he or she has no actual power to take such action.[44]

---

39 *See, e.g., Croatia v. MOL* ¶¶ 97–98; *Kim v. Uzbekistan* ¶¶ 543, 593; *Metal-Tech v. Uzbekistan* ¶ 289.

40 *See, e.g.*, The OECD Convention on Bribery: A Commentary, edited by Mark Pieth, et al, 2nd ed., 2014 ("Commentary to OECD Convention on Bribery") at 128–129; International Anti-Corruption Resource Center, Guide to Combatting Corruption & Fraud in Development Projects, available at https://guide.iacrc.org/potential-scheme-bribes-and-kickbacks/ (last accessed Apr. 15, 2019) ("IACRC Guide to Combatting Corruption") (noting that "[t]he 'thing of value' need not be money, and often is not," and providing examples of other forms of bribes).

41 *See, e.g.*, Commentary to OECD Convention on Bribery at 136–139; *Metal-Tech v. Uzbekistan* ¶¶ 286, 288–289 (finding under the applicable Uzbek law that "the timing of payment is irrelevant" and "can occur before or after the act or omission sought," and that a crime has been committed "even if no transfer is ever made").

42 FCPA Resource Guide at 12–13 (explaining that bribes paid "to secure favorable treatment, to reduce or eliminate customs duties, to obtain government action to prevent competitors from entering a market, or to circumvent a licensing or permit requirement, all satisfy the business purpose test").

43 *Id.* at 14.

44 *See, e.g.*, Explanatory Notes to UK Bribery Act of 2010 ¶ 44 (explaining that bribery is committed if a person intends to influence a foreign public official in performing his or her official functions, "even if he or she does not have authority to use the position in that way"); *Metal-Tech v. Uzbekistan* ¶ 288 (finding that it is "largely non-controversial … under

Sixth, the foreign public official need not benefit directly from the bribe. The beneficiary may instead be "another person or entity."[45] Enriching a public official's family member or an affiliated organization in order to influence the official's performance of his or her official duties therefore is equally unlawful as paying that official directly.[46]

Seventh and relatedly, bribes may be negotiated and paid indirectly. Indeed, a common method of concealing bribes is to pay consultants or contractors pursuant to sham contracts and invoices for goods and services that appear legitimate but were not actually provided.[47] Thus, while consultants and intermediaries play an important and legitimate role in international business transactions, companies must ensure that bribes are not paid on their behalf through such intermediaries. A resource guide on the FCPA published by the U.S. government therefore states:

> Many companies doing business in a foreign country retain a local individual or company to help them conduct business. Although these foreign agents may provide entirely legitimate advice regarding local customs and procedures and may help facilitate business transactions, companies should be aware of the risks involved in engaging third-party agents or intermediaries. The fact that a bribe is paid by a third party does not eliminate the potential for criminal or civil FCPA liability.[48]

---

all modern legal systems" that "an official may be bribed to take an action that he has no actual power to take").

45 U.N. Convention Against Corruption Art. 16(1).

46 *See, e.g.*, Commentary to OECD Convention on Bribery at 121 ("Thus, a businessman bribes a public official not only in the case where he pays the latter a bribe directly. He also does so when he arranges a scholarship or place at University or College for the official's son, when he gives the official's wife a fur coat, if he makes a contribution to the political party to which the official may be affiliated or contributes to the coffers of the undertaking for which the official works."); FCPA Resource Guide at 16; *Metal-Tech v. Uzbekistan* ¶¶ 288–289.

47 *See, e.g.*, FCPA Resource Guide at 14; IACRC Guide to Combatting Corruption (stating that "payments through subcontractors or local agents, recorded on the contractor's books as legitimate fees and commissions … is the most common method used by large companies to pay and conceal bribes," and that "[c]ash for corrupt payments can be generated by raising false invoices for goods, works, or services that were not performed, and turning the payments into cash"); Mark Pieth, "Contractual Freedom v. Public Policy Considerations in Arbitration," *in* PRIVATE LAW, NATIONAL-GLOBAL-COMPARATIVE, Büchler, Müller-Chen (eds.), 2011 at 1376 (describing intermediaries as "the most prominent trouble zone").

48 FCPA Resource Guide at 21–22.

The commentary to the OECD Convention on Combating Bribery of Foreign Public Officials in International Business Transactions likewise notes that consultants and other third parties commonly are engaged during the investment or procurement process at "precisely the moments when decisions by the foreign public official are called for."[49] It thus warns investors about the risks of indirect bribery, observing that "[n]either legal nor natural persons can evade liability by 'delegating' bribery to others."[50]

Eighth, while the bribe must be intended for a foreign public official to take or refrain from taking official action in the exercise of his or her official duties, there is an important exception: persons who exercise foreign State authority without a specific legal basis, on a *de facto* basis, generally are considered public officials subject to anti-bribery laws.[51]

For example, the Swiss Federal Criminal Court found that a former manager of SNC Lavalin had paid bribes to Saadi Gaddafi, the son of the longtime leader of Libya, Colonel Muammar Gaddafi, in violation of the anti-bribery prohibitions of the Swiss Criminal Code. The court determined, among other things, that the official political system in Libya "was nothing but a façade" and that actual power "depended directly on personal or family relations" with Colonel Gaddafi.[52] The court accordingly held that Saadi Gaddafi was in fact a public official who had been paid bribes, not based on the limited State functions he formally could exercise through his official position in the government, but rather because he was a member of the ruling family and therefore had the *de facto* power to take decisions on behalf of the State.[53]

Similarly, three global telecommunications companies and their subsidiaries pled guilty in the United States and paid a total of US$ 2.61 billion in penalties and disgorgement of profits to U.S., Dutch, and Swedish authorities for paying bribes to Gulnara Karimova, the daughter of the longtime President of the Republic of Uzbekistan, Islam Karimov.[54] The U.S. Department of Justice

49 Commentary to OECD Convention on Bribery at 154.

50 *Id.* at 148.

51 *Id.* at 86–87.

52 Swiss Federal Criminal Court, SK.2014.24, Decision dated Oct. 1, 2014 against Riadh Ben Aïssa, former manager of SNC Lavalin, accused of bribing in Libya at 3 (translation) ("*Le système politique official n'était qu'une façade; les hauts fonctionnaires des institutions officielles ne disposaient guère de véritables compétences de décision et d'organisation et exécutaient les décisions prises par les personnes disposant du pouvoir effectif. Le pouvoir et l'influence dépendaient directement des relations personnelles ou familiales avec M.*").

53 *Id.* at 3–4.

54 *United States of America v. VimpelCom Ltd. and Unitel*, Criminal Case No. 16-cr-137-ER, S.D.N.Y. ("*U.S. v. VimpelCom and Unitel*"), Court Transcript dated Feb. 18, 2016; *id.* Plea Agreement dated Feb. 22, 2016; *id.* Deferred Prosecution Agreement dated Feb. 22, 2016;

also has indicted Ms. Karimova for demanding approximately US$ 866 million in bribes to exert "her influence over the Uzbek government to ensure that the three telecommunications companies and their subsidiaries acquired telecommunications licenses, which, under Uzbek law, could not be purchased or transferred by private entities, and also to allow the telecommunications companies to enter, and continue to operate in, the telecommunications market in Uzbekistan."[55] Thus, as with Colonel Gaddafi's son, the authorities charged that Ms. Karimova was a public official, not merely because she held formal positions in Uzbekistan's Ministry of Foreign Affairs, but because she *de facto* exercised control over government organs and agencies while her father ruled the country.[56]

---

*Securities & Exchange Commission v. VimpelCom Ltd.*, Civil Case No. 16-cv-1266-VM, S.D.N.Y., Final Judgment dated Feb. 22, 2016; *United States of America v. Unitel*, Criminal Case No. 16-cr-137-ER, S.D.N.Y., Criminal Judgment dated Feb. 26, 2016; *United States of America v. Telia Company AB*, Criminal Case No. 1:17-cr-00581-GBD, S.D N.Y., Criminal Information dated Sept. 21, 2017, Deferred Prosecution Agreement dated Sept. 21, 2017; *United States of America v. Mobile TeleSystems PJSC*, Criminal Case No. 19-cr-00167-JPO, S.D.N.Y., Criminal Information dated Mar. 6, 2019; *In re Mobile TeleSystems PJSC*, File No. 3-19022, SEC, Order Instituting Cease-and-Desist Proceedings dated Mar. 6, 2019.

55 *United States of America v. Karimova*, Criminal Case No. 19-cr-00165-KMW, S.D.N.Y., Indictment dated Mar. 7, 2019 at 1–2. *See also* "Former Uzbek Government Official and Uzbek Telecommunications Executive Charged in Bribery and Money Laundering Scheme Involving the Payment of Nearly $1 Billion in Bribes," U.S. Department of Justice, U.S. Attorney's Office, Press Release dated Mar. 7, 2019 (Brian Benczkowski, the Assistant Attorney General for the Criminal Division of the Department of Justice, stating that "Gulnara Karimova stands accused of exploiting her official position to solicit and accept more than $865 million in bribes from three publicly traded telecom companies, and then laundering those bribes through the U.S. financial system").

56 *See, e.g.*, Swiss Federal Criminal Court, R.R.2013.205 + R.R.2013.206, Decision dated Nov. 5, 2013 ("Thus, as in the case of officials ..., members of an authority may also exist in law or in fact. In the latter case, there is no service relationship and they exercise their power solely due to their situation. In the present case, and in particular in view of the various diplomatic charges exerted to date by Gulnara Karimova on behalf of Uzbekistan ..., a country governed by her own father, it is not unreasonable to consider that she exercises de facto power solely on the basis of her situation and that she is similar to a member of an authority.") (translation) ("*Ainsi, les membres d'une autorité peuvent, à l'instar de ce qui est retenu pour les fonctionnaires ..., eux aussi exister de droit ou de fait Dans ce dernier cas, il n'existe aucun rapport de service et ils exercent leur pouvoir de par leur seule situation. En l'espèce, et notamment au vu des diverses charges diplomatiques exercées à ce jour par Gulnara Karimova pour le compte de l'Ouzbékistan ... , pays dirigé par le propre père de cette dernière, il n'est pas insoutenable de retenir qu'elle exerce un pouvoir de fait de par sa seule situation, et qu'elle puisse être assimilée à un membre d'une autorité.*"); *U.S. v. VimpelCom and Unitel*, Deferred Prosecution Agreement dated Feb. 22, 2016 at 7 (determining that Ms. Karimova was a "Public official in a high-level decision-making position" under § 2C.1.1 of the U.S. sentencing guidelines); United States Sentencing Commission,

Other courts and tribunals, by contrast, have dismissed allegations of bribery based on a narrow and formalistic view that a "public official" must have the authority by law to take official action and does not include the *de facto* exercise of such authority.[57]

Finally, bribery has an element of criminal intent or *mens rea*. Under the U.N. Convention against Corruption, bribery must be "committed intentionally."[58] Likewise, under the FCPA, criminal liability is limited to individuals who act "willfully," and while proof of willfulness is not required for civil liability or for corporate criminal liability, proof of corrupt intent is.[59]

For purposes of satisfying this *mens rea* requirement, it is sufficient to show that the accused individual acted "with a bad purpose" and knew generally that his or her conduct was unlawful.[60] Moreover, intention or *mens rea* will be inferred if the individual willfully disregarded facts indicating a high probability that a subordinate or intermediary was engaged in bribery.[61] Ignorance is not a defense in those circumstances as anti-bribery laws "impose liability not only on those with actual knowledge of wrongdoing, but also on those who purposefully avoid actual knowledge."[62]

With these considerations in mind, we turn next to the burden and standard of proof for allegations of corruption in international arbitration.

---

Guidelines Manual dated Nov. 1, 2015 at 134–135 ("'Public official' shall be construed broadly and includes," among other things, an individual who, although not otherwise covered, "(i) is in a position of public trust with official responsibility for carrying out a government program or policy; (ii) acts under color of law or official right; or (iii) participates so substantially in government operations as to possess de facto authority to make governmental decisions ...").

57 *See, e.g., Kim v. Uzbekistan* ¶¶ 569–577 (finding that Gulnara Karimova was not a public official capable of being bribed); Stockholm District Court, Section 4, Goal no. B 12201-17, B 12203-17, Judgment dated Feb. 15, 2019 (same). The *Kim* tribunal's jurisdictional decision has not been incorporated in a final award and thus may still be subject to future challenge.

58 U.N. Convention Against Corruption, Art. 16(1).

59 *Compare* 15 U.S. Code § 78dd-2(g)(2)(A) *with* 15 U.S. Code § 78dd-3(e)(2)(A). *See also* FCPA Resource Guide at 14.

60 *Id.* at 14.

61 *Id.* at 22, 65, 94, 97, 99; Commentary to OECD Convention on Bribery at 150–151.

62 FCPA Resource Guide at 22 ("[T]he so-called 'head-in-the-sand' problem—variously described in the pertinent authorities as 'conscious disregard,' 'willful blindness' or 'deliberate ignorance'—should be covered so that management officials could not take refuge from the Act's prohibitions by their unwarranted obliviousness to any action (or inaction), language or other 'signaling device' that should reasonably alert them of the 'high probability' of an FCPA violation.").

## IV The Burden and Standard of Proof for Allegations of Corruption

The burden and standard of proof have been described as "one of the most contentious problems of corruption cases in arbitral practice."[63] As discussed below, the rules relating to the burden and standard of proof may be summarized as follows: (1) the burden of proof is on the party alleging corruption to prove it; (2) courts and tribunals differ as to the applicable standard of proof, although the majority require more compelling evidence to prove corruption; (3) corruption nevertheless may be proven through circumstantial, rather than direct, evidence; and (4) tribunals may draw adverse inferences against either party for failing to produce evidence.

### 4.1 *The Burden of Proof Is on the Party Alleging Corruption*

The burden of proof describes the legal burden borne by the party that must persuade the tribunal in order to prevail on its entire case or a particular issue.[64]

According to the jurisprudence of the International Court of Justice ("ICJ"), whichever party alleges a fact has the burden of proving it, a principle derived from the Latin maxim *onus probandi incumbit actori*.[65] Both the UNCITRAL arbitration rules and the Iran-United States Claims Tribunal rules of procedure similarly provide: "Each party shall have the burden of proving the facts relied on to support its claim or defence."[66] While the ICSID arbitration rules and the International Chamber of Commerce ("ICC") arbitration rules are both silent as to the burden of proof, tribunals in cases arising under these rules also have observed that "[i]t is a well-established rule in international adjudication that

---

63 Peter Muchlinski, Federico Ortino and Christoph Schreuer, THE OXFORD HANDBOOK OF INTERNATIONAL INVESTMENT LAW (2008), Oxford University Press at 604; Michael Hwang and Kevin Lim, "Corruption in Arbitration—Law and Reality," Asian International Arbitration Journal, Kluwer Law International 2012, Vol. 8, Issue 1 at 1–119.

64 *Rompetrol Group N.V. v. Romania*, ICSID Case No. ARB/06/3, Award dated May 6, 2013 ("*Rompetrol v. Romania*") ¶ 178.

65 *See, e.g., Pulp Mills (Argentina v. Uruguay)*, Judgment, ICJ Reports 2010 ¶ 162 ("[I]n accordance with the well-established principle of *onus probandi imcumbit actori*, it is the duty of the party which asserts certain facts to establish the existence of such facts This principle which has been consistently upheld by the Court applies to the assertions of fact both by the Applicant and the Respondent."). *See also* Peter Tomka and Vincent-Joel Proulx, *The Evidentiary Practice of the World Court*, National University of Singapore, Working Paper 2015/010, Dec. 2015 at 16 (explaining that this "rule of thumb" is "often reiterated" by the Court and "resembles that found in most domestic judicial proceedings on civil matters").

66 UNCITRAL Arbitration Rules (2013) Art. 27.1; Iran-United States Claims Tribunal Rules of Procedure dated 1983 Art. 24.1.

the burden of proof lies with the party alleging a fact, whether it is the claimant or the respondent."[67]

Applying this straightforward rule, the party alleging corruption has the burden of proving it.[68] The other party has no legal burden to disprove the allegation.

The ICSID tribunal in *AAPL v. Sri Lanka* suggested, however, that the burden of proof may "shift" in certain circumstances. According to the *AAPL* tribunal, it is a principle of international law that cases are decided based "on the strength of the evidence produced by both parties," and if a party "'adduces some evidence which prima facie supports his allegation, the burden of proof shifts to his opponent.'"[69]

Certain tribunals have agreed with *AAPL* that the burden of proof may shift in certain circumstances. In *Karkey v. Pakistan*, for example, the ICSID tribunal held that Pakistan had the burden to prove its allegations of corruption and fraud "pursuant to the well-established principle *onus probandi incumbit actori* (the party that asserts must prove)," and that the burden of proof may shift to Karkey "should the Tribunal be satisfied that there is unequivocal (or unambiguous) *prima facie* evidence in this regard."[70]

---

67 *Saipem S.p.A. v. The People's Republic of Bangladesh*, ICSID Case No. ARB/05/7, Award dated June 30, 2009 ¶ 113. *See also, e.g., Metal-Tech v. Uzbekistan* ¶ 237 ("The principle that each party has the burden of proving the facts on which it relies is widely recognized and applied by international courts and tribunals.").

68 *See, e.g., EDF (Services) Limited v. Romania*, ICSID Case No. ARB/05/16, Award dated Oct. 8, 2009 ("*EDF v. Romania*") ¶ 232; *Liman Caspian Oil BV and NCL Dutch Investment BV v. Republic of Kazakhstan*, ICSID Case No. ARB/07/14, Excerpts of Award dated June 22, 2010 ("*Liman v. Kazakhstan*") ¶¶ 422–423; *Kim v. Uzbekistan* ¶ 557. White & Case LLP represented Romania in *EDF v. Romania.*

69 *Asian Agricultural Products Ltd. v. Republic of Sri Lanka*, ICSID Case No. ARB/87/3, Award dated June 27, 1990 ("*AAPL v. Sri Lanka*") ¶ 56 (Rule L).

70 *Karkey Karadeniz Elektrik Uretim A.S. v. Islamic Republic of Pakistan*, ICSID Case No. ARB/13/1, Award dated Aug. 22, 2017 ("*Karkey v. Pakistan*") ¶ 497. For similar observations in other contexts, *see, e.g., Tradex Hellas S.A. v. Republic of Albania*, ICSID Case No. ARB/94/2, Award dated Apr. 29, 1999 ¶ 84; *Middle East Cement Shipping and Handling Co. S.A. v. Arab Republic of Egypt*, ICSID Case No. ARB/99/6, Award dated Apr. 12, 2002 ¶ 94; *Marvin Roy Feldman Karpa v. United Mexican States*, ICSID Case No ARB(AF)/99/1, Award dated Dec. 16, 2002 ¶¶ 177–178; *Ioan Micula, Viorel Micula, SC European Food SA, SC Starmill SRL and SC Multipack SRL v. Romania*, ICSID Case No ARB/05/20, Decision on Jurisdiction and Admissibility dated Sept. 24, 2008 ¶ 96; *Alpha Projektholding GmbH v. Ukraine*, ICSID Case No. ARB/07/16, Award dated Nov. 8, 2010 ¶ 236; *Tza Yap Shum v. Republic of Peru*, ICSID Case No ARB/07/6, Award dated July 7, 2011 ¶ 73.

Several ICC tribunals have made similar observations.[71] Thus, in ICC Case No. 6497, the tribunal held that, if the party alleging corruption proffers "some relevant evidence for its allegations, without these elements being really conclusive," then "the arbitral tribunal may exceptionally request the other party to bring some counter-evidence, if such task is possible and not too burdensome."[72] The tribunal further commented that, if that party failed to proffer such counter-evidence, then "the arbitral tribunal may conclude that the facts alleged are proven."[73] The tribunal noted, however, that "such change in the burden of proof is only to be made in special circumstances and for very good reasons."[74]

Notwithstanding these comments, none of these tribunals actually shifted the burden of proof to the party accused of corruption. In *Karkey*, the tribunal found that Pakistan had merely raised questions that were insufficient to shift Pakistan's burden of proving its allegations, "so as to require Karkey to exonerate itself."[75] As discussed by Alexis Mourre, the President of the ICC International Court of Arbitration, the ICC tribunals likewise did not "really shift the burden of proof," but instead drew "adverse inferences from the refusal of a party to cooperate fully with the procedure."[76] We discuss such adverse inferences below.[77]

Shifting the burden of proof to the party accused of corruption to exonerate itself is problematic for several reasons. First, while "prima facie" evidence derives from a Latin phrase meaning "at first sight" and is used in certain legal systems to refer to evidence that creates a presumption requiring the other party to rebut it, "[i]nternational arbitration is not an inquisitorial system where the [t]ribunal establishes the facts for a denunciating party, nor a

---

71 *See, e.g.*, ICC Case No. 6497, Award of 1994, *Yearbook of Commercial Arbitration* 24a (1999) ("ICC Case No. 6497") ¶ 4; ICC Case No. 12990, Award dated Dec. 2005, *ICC Bulletin (Supplement)* 24 (2013) ("ICC Case No. 12990").

72 ICC Case No. 6497 ¶ 4.

73 *Id.*

74 *Id.*

75 *Karkey v. Pakistan* ¶ 521.

76 Alexis Mourre, "Arbitration in Criminal Law: Reflections on the Duties of the Arbitrator," Arbitration International 22:1 dated 2006 ("Mourre, Arbitration in Criminal Law") at 95, 103. *See also, e.g.*, Vera van Houtte, "Adverse Inferences in International Arbitration," *in* WRITTEN EVIDENCE AND DISCOVERY IN INTERNATIONAL ARBITRATION: NEW ISSUES AND TENDENCIES, Teresa Giovannini and Alexis Mourre (eds) dated 2009 at 196 ("van Houtte, Adverse Inferences") (agreeing with Jeremy Sharpe s observation that "it is not the burden of proof but the 'burden of production' or the 'evidential burden' that is alleviated or shifted in these cases, leaving the 'burden of proof' rule of *actori incumbit probatio* intact.").

77 *See infra* § 4.4.

system where it is sufficient to make a *prima facie* case relying on the opponent to rebut that case."[78]

Second, there are serious due process concerns with requiring the accused party to prove it did nothing wrong.[79] While corruption is "notoriously difficult to prove since, typically, there is little or no physical evidence,"[80] requiring a party to prove the absence of corruption would be equally (if not more) difficult and would contravene the presumption of innocence that exists in most legal systems. The ICSID tribunal in *Siag v. Egypt* accordingly refused to shift the burden of proof and held that "the reversal of the burden of proof may make it almost impossible for the allegedly fraudulent party to defend itself, thus violating due process standards."[81]

Third, the burden of proof is a "persuasive burden" that is distinct from the obligation of both parties to produce evidence.[82] Bin Cheng thus observes in his treatise on general principles of international law that a "Party having the burden of proof must not only bring evidence in support of his allegations, but must convince the Tribunal of their truth, lest they be disregarded for want, or insufficiency, of proof."[83] *Phipson on Evidence* likewise observes that only one party bears the burden of proving any particular issue, and if that party fails

78 *Jan Oostergetel and Theodora Laurentius v. The Slovak Republic*, UNCITRAL, Final Award dated Apr. 23, 2012 ("*Oostergetel v. Slovak Republic*") ¶ 148. *See also Metal-Tech v. Uzbekistan* ¶ 238 ("Rules establishing presumptions or shifting the burden of proof are generally deemed to be part of the *lex causae*. In the present case, the *lex causae* is essentially the BIT, which provides no rules for shifting the burden of proof or establishing presumptions.").

79 Alexis Mourre, Arbitration in Criminal Law at 95, 103 (observing that shifting the burden of proof in corruption cases "does not seem to be acceptable or compatible with the right to a fair trial").

80 *EDF v. Romania* ¶ 221. *See also Metal-Tech v. Uzbekistan* ¶ 243 (observing that "corruption is by essence difficult to establish"); *Oriekhov v. Union des Associations Européennes de Football (UEFA)*, CAS 2010/A/2172, Award dated Jan. 18, 2011 ¶ 54 (observing that "corruption is, by nature, concealed as the parties involved will seek to use evasive means to ensure that they leave no trail of their wrongdoing"); Joseph E. Stiglitz and Mark Pieth, *Overcoming the Shadow Economy*, Friedrich Ebert Stiftung (Nov. 2016) at 3 (describing the difficulty of tracing corrupt payments made in "secrecy havens" "in which global financial flows were hidden in ways that not even those entrusted with enforcing the laws and regulations of countries around the world could detect").

81 *Waguih George Siag and Clorinda Vecchi v. The Arab Republic of Egypt*, ICSID Case No. ARB/05/15, Award dated June 1, 2009 ("*Siag v. Egypt*") ¶¶ 316–317.

82 Hodge Malek, Jonathan Auburn, and Roderick Bagshaw, PHIPSON ON EVIDENCE § 6-02 (17th ed. 2009) ("Phipson on Evidence"); Tapper and Colin, CROSS AND TAPPER ON EVIDENCE 121 (12th ed. 2010) ("Cross and Tapper on Evidence").

83 Bin Cheng, GENERAL PRINCIPLES OF LAW AS APPLIED BY INTERNATIONAL COURTS AND TRIBUNAL 329–331 (1987) ("Cheng, General Principles of Law"). *See also*

to discharge its burden, it "will lose on the issue in question."[84] The treatise further comments that it therefore "is wrong to speak of the persuasive burden shifting during the course of the trial."[85] And *Cross and Tapper on Evidence* confirms that, "[o]n any one issue, there can be only ... one persuasive burden," which "can be borne by only one party."[86]

Consistent with these observations, in *Apotex v. United States*, an ICSID additional facility arbitration arising under the North American Free Trade Agreement ("NAFTA"), the tribunal remarked that the "legal burden of proof" "never shifts."[87] The ICSID tribunal in the resubmitted *Fraport v. Philippines* arbitration similarly held that the Philippines had the burden of proving its jurisdictional objections, and that while Fraport would need to provide rebuttal evidence if the Philippines supported its objections with prima facie evidence, even in such a circumstance the Philippines "retains the ultimate burden to prove its jurisdictional objections."[88]

The ICSID tribunal in *Rompetrol v. Romania* observed, moreover, "that the burden of proof is absolute," and that "if, according to basic principle, it is for the one party, or for the other, to establish a particular factual assertion, that will remain the position throughout the forensic process, starting from when the assertion is first put forward and all the way through to the end."[89] The *Rompetrol* tribunal thus confirmed that the burden of proof does not shift:

> Operating within an international system characterised by principle rather than procedural formality, the Tribunal is not enamoured of arguments setting out to show that a burden of proof can under certain circumstances shift from the party that originally bore it to the other party, and then perhaps in appropriate circumstances shift back again

---

*Ampal-American Israel Corporation and others v. Arab Republic of Egypt*, ICSID Case No. ARB/12/11, Decision on Jurisdiction dated Feb. 1, 2016 ¶ 219; *AAPL v. Sri Lanka* ¶ 56.

84 Phipson on Evidence §§ 6-02, 6-03.

85 *Id.* § 6-03.

86 Cross and Tapper on Evidence at 121.

87 *Apotex Holdings Inc. and Apotex Inc. v. United States of America*, ICSID Case No. ARB(AF)12/1, Award dated Aug. 25, 2014 ¶ 8.8 (distinguishing the "legal burden of proof" with the obligation to produce evidence or "evidential burden of proof," which "can shift from one party to another, depending upon the state of the evidence").

88 *Fraport AG Frankfurt Airport Services Worldwide v. Republic of the Philippines*, ICSID Case No. ARB/11/12, Award dated Dec. 10, 2014 ("*Fraport v. Philippines II*") ¶ 299 (affirming "the well-established rule of *onus probandi incumbit actori*," whereby "the burden of proof rests upon the party that is asserting affirmatively a claim or defense"). White & Case LLP represented the Republic of Philippines in both arbitrations brought by Fraport.

89 *Rompetrol v. Romania* ¶ 178.

to the original party. To the mind of the Tribunal, arguments of that kind confuse, unhelpfully, the separate questions of who has to prove a particular assertion and whether that assertion has in fact been proved on the evidence.[90]

The ICSID tribunal in *Union Fenosa v. Egypt* accordingly stated: "The legal burden of proving corruption rests upon the party alleging corruption; and it is not discharged by placing the burden on the adverse party to prove the absence of corruption."[91] Thus, as these authorities confirm, the party alleging corruption has the burden of proving it, and its opponent does not bear any "burden of (dis)proof."[92]

### 4.2 *Most Courts and Tribunals Require More Compelling Evidence to Prove Corruption and Fraud*

The next issue is what standard of proof applies to allegations of corruption. The standard of proof describes the extent of evidence needed for a party to prove a particular allegation or its case as a whole and thus meet its burden of proof.[93] We set out below the approach taken by national courts and international tribunals with regard to the standard of proof.

#### 4.2.1 The Standard of Proof Applied by National Courts

In countries based on a civil law system, the judge is the trier of fact and has freedom in assessing the evidence. The judge is not bound by any strict standard of proof and may decide both civil and criminal matters based on his or her inner conviction (*l'intime conviction du juge*).[94] Civil claims arising out of alleged crimes consequently may be joined to criminal proceedings as both

90 *Id.*

91 *Union Fenosa Gas, S.A. v. Arab Republic of Egypt*, ICSID Case No. ARB/14/4, Award dated Aug. 31, 2018 ("*Union Fenosa v. Egypt*") ¶ 7.113.

92 *Rompetrol v. Romania* ¶ 179 (rejecting the suggestion that either party bore a "burden of (dis)proof" and deciding it could "safely rest, so far as the burden of proof is concerned, on the widely accepted international principle that a party in litigation bears the burden of proving the facts relied on to support its claim or defence").

93 *See, e.g.*, Phipson on Evidence § 6-01 ("The phrase 'standard of proof' is used to describe the degree to which the proof must be established."); *Rompetrol v. Romania* ¶ 178 (observing that "the standard of proof defines how much evidence is needed to establish either an individual issue or the party's case as a whole").

94 Kevin Clermont and Emily Sherwin, "A Comparative View of Standards of Proof," 50 AM. J. COMP. L. 243, 255–56 (2002) (providing a historical analysis of the standard of proof in both civil law and common law jurisdictions). *See also* Kevin Clermont, "Standards of Proof Revisited," 33 VERMONT LAW REV. 469, 471 (2009).

matters will be decided based on the judge's inner conviction.[95] Accordingly, while the inner conviction is a flexible standard that may vary depending on the judge, commentators have suggested that the level of persuasion required is typically high.[96]

In countries based on a common law system, by contrast, different standards of proof apply in civil and criminal proceedings. The standard of proof in civil proceedings is usually the "preponderance of evidence" or "balance of probabilities," which requires proof that the facts alleged are more likely true than not true.[97] A much higher standard of proof "beyond a reasonable doubt" applies in criminal cases. That standard seeks to protect against wrongful convictions and therefore requires "proof coming as close to certainty as is humanly possible."[98]

The United States also recognizes a third standard of proof, often described as "clear and convincing evidence," that is higher than a preponderance of evidence but not as high as proof beyond a reasonable doubt. The "clear and convincing evidence" standard requires proof that the facts alleged are not merely probable, but are in fact highly probable so as to establish "a firm belief or conviction that the allegations in question are true."[99] U.S. courts apply this standard under the due process clause of the Fourteenth Amendment to the U.S. Constitution in proceedings where the individual interests at stake are more consequential than the loss of money, such as involuntary commitment, denaturalization, deportation, or the irrevocable termination of parental rights.[100] U.S. courts also require clear and convincing evidence for civil claims alleging serious illegality such as fraud, undue influence, and corruption.[101]

---

95 Jean-Marc Baissus, "Common v. Continental: A Reaction to Mr. Evan Whitton's 1998 Murdoch Law School Address," 5 MURDOCH U. ELEC. J.L No. 4 (Dec. 1998) ¶ 77.

96 *See, e.g.*, Margaret Moses, THE PRINCIPLES AND PRACTICE OF INTERNATIONAL COMMERCIAL ARBITRATION (2nd ed. 2012) 174; Caroline Buisman, Myriam Bouazdi, and Matteo Costi, "Principles of Civil Law," *in* PRINCIPLES OF EVIDENCE IN INTERNATIONAL CRIMINAL JUSTICE, Karim Khan, Caroline Buisman, and Christopher Gosnell eds., 2010 at 37 (comparing *l'intime conviction du juge* to the beyond reasonable doubt standard applicable in criminal cases in common law countries); Mark Schweizer, "The Civil Standard of Proof—What Is It, Actually?" *Max Planck Institute for Research on Collective Goods* (2013) at 12.

97 AMERICAN JURISPRUDENCE, 29 AM. JUR. 2D EVIDENCE § 173 (United States) ("American Jurisprudence on Evidence"); Cross and Tapper on Evidence at 165.

98 American Jurisprudence on Evidence § 173. *See also* Cross and Tapper on Evidence at 158.

99 American Jurisprudence on Evidence § 173.

100 American Jurisprudence on Evidence § 179.

101 American Jurisprudence on Evidence §§ 173, 179. *See also, e.g.*, John Terrence A. Rosenthal and Robert T. Alter, "Clear and Convincing to Whom? The False Claims Act And Its Burden of Proof Standard: Why the Government Needs a Big Stick," 75 NOTRE DAME L.

In contrast to the U.S., other common law jurisdictions, such as England, apply the ordinary "balance of probabilities" standard in all civil proceedings regardless of the subject matter of the dispute.[102] In rejecting calls for an intermediate standard of proof, the U.K. House of Lords has held that "a 'high civil balance of probabilities' is an unfortunate mixed metaphor. The civil standard of proof always means more likely than not. The only higher degree of probability required by the law is the criminal standard."[103] While the standard of proof in civil proceedings in England accordingly is "finite and unvarying,"[104] the House of Lords has observed that certain allegations require more rigorous examination:

> [I]n some contexts a court or tribunal has to look at the facts more critically or anxiously than in others before it can be satisfied to the requisite standard.... Situations which make such heightened examination necessary may be the inherent unlikelihood of the occurrence taking place ..., the seriousness of the allegation to be proved or, in some cases, the consequences which could follow from acceptance of proof of the relevant fact. The seriousness of the allegation requires no elaboration: a tribunal of fact will look closely into the facts grounding an allegation of fraud before accepting that it has been established. The seriousness of consequences is another facet of the same proposition....[105]

The House of Lords further has observed that fraud is "usually less likely than negligence" and, more generally, that "the more serious the allegation the less likely it is that the event occurred and, hence, the stronger should be the evidence before the court concludes that the allegation is established on the balance of probability."[106] For these reasons, the House of Lords has held that "cogent evidence is generally required to satisfy a civil tribunal that a

REV. 1409, 1439–40 (2000) (explaining that the higher standard requires civil plaintiffs alleging illegality "to go above and beyond the requirements of courts of law because the potential equitable remedies could be so drastic in scope").

102 Cross and Tapper on Evidence at 165.

103 *Secretary of State for the Home Department v. Rehman (AP)* [2001] UKHL 47 ¶ 55; *In re Doherty* [2008] UKHL 33 ¶ 26 (same).

104 *In re Doherty* [2008] UKHL 33 ¶ 28.

105 *Id.* (further observing that these factors "do not require a different standard of proof or a specially cogent standard of evidence, merely appropriately careful consideration by the tribunal before it is satisfied of the matter which has to be established").

106 *Re H (Minors)* [1996] AC 563, 586. *Id.* ("The more improbable the event, the stronger must be the evidence that it did occur before, on the balance of probability, its occurrence will be established.").

person has been fraudulent or behaved in some other reprehensible manner," although "the question is always whether the tribunal thinks it more probable than not."[107]

The approach in Australia is similar. In a divorce case in the 1930s, the High Court of Australia observed that, "[i]n a serious matter like a charge of adultery the satisfaction of a just and prudent mind cannot be produced by slender and exiguous proofs or circumstances pointing with a wavering finger to an affirmative conclusion."[108] The court held that the nature of the allegation of adultery required "as a matter of common sense and worldly wisdom the careful weighing of testimony, the close examination of facts proved as a basis of inference and a comfortable satisfaction that the tribunal has reached both a correct and just conclusion."[109] Thus, while there is no intermediate standard of proof in Australia, the High Court has clarified that judges may require stronger evidence to establish that allegations of serious misconduct, including crimes such as fraud and corruption, are more probable than not:

> The ordinary standard of proof required of a party who bears the onus in civil litigation in this country is proof on the balance of probabilities. That remains so even where the matter to be proved involves criminal conduct or fraud. On the other hand, the strength of the evidence necessary to establish a fact or facts on the balance of probabilities may vary according to the nature of what it is sought to prove. Thus, authoritative statements have often been made to the effect that clear or cogent or strict proof is necessary 'where so serious a matter as fraud is to be found'. Statements to that effect should not, however, be understood as directed to the standard of proof. Rather, they should be understood as merely reflecting a conventional perception that members of our society do not ordinarily engage in fraudulent or criminal conduct and a judicial approach that a court should not lightly make a finding that, on the balance of probabilities, a party to civil litigation has been guilty of such conduct.[110]

---

107 *Secretary of State for the Home Department v. Rehman (AP)* [2001] UKHL 17 ¶ 55. *See also, e.g.*, Cross and Tapper on Evidence at 165.

108 *Briginshaw v. Briginshaw* (1938) 60 CLR 336, 350.

109 *Id.*

110 *Neat Holdings Pty Ltd v. Karajan Holdings Pty Ltd.* (1992) 67 ALJR 170. *See also Evidence Act 1995* § 140 (Cth and NSW) (allowing judges to take into account "the nature of the cause of action, the nature of the subject-matter, and the gravity of the matters alleged in finding if a case has been proved on the balance of probabilities"); C.R. Williams, "Burdens and Standards in Civil Litigation," 25 SYDNEY L. REV. 165, 182–183 (2003).

Thus, despite using different labels for the standard or proof, the U.S., England, and Australia all require more compelling evidence to establish civil claims based on allegations of corruption or fraud.

### 4.2.2 The Standard of Proof Applied by International Courts and Tribunals

Arbitral rules typically do not impose any strict standard of proof. The ICC arbitration rules, for example, are silent with regard to the standard of proof and the assessment of evidence more generally. Other leading arbitral rules contain substantially identical provisions granting broad discretion to tribunals to resolve evidentiary issues as the list below shows:

- International Bar Association ("IBA") Rules on the Taking of Evidence Article 9.1: "The Arbitral Tribunal shall determine the admissibility, relevance, materiality and weight of evidence."
- ICSID Arbitration Rule 34: "The Tribunal shall be the judge of the admissibility of any evidence adduced and of its probative value."
- UNCITRAL Model Law Article 19.2: "The power conferred upon the arbitral tribunal includes the power to determine the admissibility, relevance, materiality and weight of any evidence."
- UNCITRAL Arbitration Rule 27.4: "The arbitral tribunal shall determine the admissibility, relevance, materiality and weight of the evidence offered."
- Cairo Regional Centre for International Commercial Arbitration Article 27.4: "The arbitral tribunal shall determine the admissibility, relevance, materiality and weight of the evidence offered."
- Hong Kong International Arbitration Centre Article 22.2: "The arbitral tribunal shall determine the admissibility, relevance, materiality and weight of the evidence, including whether to apply strict rules of evidence."
- Iran-U.S. Claims Tribunal Article 25.6: "The arbitral tribunal shall determine the admissibility, relevance, materiality and weight of the evidence offered."
- London Court of International Arbitration Article 22.1(vi): "The Arbitral Tribunal shall have the power … to decide whether or not to apply any strict rules of evidence (or any other rules) as to the admissibility, relevance or weight of any material tended by a party on any issue of fact or expert opinion…."
- Stockholm Chamber of Commerce ("SCC") Article 31.1: "The admissibility, relevance, materiality and weight of evidence shall be for the Arbitral Tribunal to determine."
- Swiss Rules of International Arbitration Article 24.2: "The arbitral tribunal shall determine the admissibility, relevance, materiality, and weight of the evidence."

– World Intellectual Property Organization Article 50(a): "The Tribunal shall determine the admissibility, relevance, materiality and weight of evidence."

In the absence of a precise rule establishing the standard of proof, tribunals in commercial arbitrations determine the standard based on the applicable law. The choice of that law may depend, in turn, on the tribunal's determination as to whether the standard of proof is a procedural issue subject to the procedural law of the arbitral seat (*lex arbitri*), a substantive issue subject to the law governing the underlying substantive issues (*lex causae*), or subject to some international standard. Tribunals have issued conflicting decisions on this issue.[111]

Tribunals in investment arbitrations have held that the rules of evidence "are neither rigid nor technical" and entrust tribunals with "a large measure of discretion over how the relevant facts are to be found and to be proved."[112] Tribunals in investment arbitrations therefore freely assess the evidence and are not bound to apply any particular standard of proof.[113]

In practice, most international courts and tribunals have held that the standard of proof for ordinary allegations is the "preponderance of evidence" or the "balance of probabilities."[114] For "allegations of particular gravity," such as

---

111 *See, e.g.*, Andrea J. Menaker and Brody K. Greenwald, "Proving Corruption in International Arbitration: Who Has the Burden and How Can it Be Met?," *in* ADDRESSING ISSUES OF CORRUPTION IN COMMERCIAL INVESTMENT ARBITRATION 78–79 (International Chamber of Commerce ed., 2014) (providing examples).

112 *Rompetrol v. Romania* ¶ 181 (further observing "that an ICSID tribunal is endowed with the independent power to determine, within the context provided by the circumstances of the dispute before it, whether particular evidence or kinds of evidence should be admitted or excluded, what weight (if any) should be given to particular items of evidence so admitted, whether it would like to see further evidence of any particular kind on any issue arising in the case, and so on and so forth"). *See also, e.g.*, *Adem Dogan v. Turkmenistan*, ICSID Case No. ARB/09/9, Decision on Annulment dated Jan. 15, 2016 ¶ 165 ("A tribunal has broad discretion when evaluating the probative value of evidence. As stated by Professor Schreuer 'ICSID arbitration is not governed by formal rules nor by national laws on evidence. ICSID tribunals have full discretion in assessing the probative value of any piece of evidence introduced before them.'").

113 *See, e.g.*, *Unglaube v. Republic of Costa Rica*, ICSID Case No. ARB/08/1, Award dated May 16, 2012 ¶ 34 ("Because no single precise standard has been articulated, tribunals ultimately exercise discretion in this area.").

114 Nathan D. O'Malley, RULES OF EVIDENCE IN INTERNATIONAL ARBITRATION: AN ANNOTATED GUIDE 208–212 (2012) ("O'Malley, Rules of Evidence") (observing that the balance of probabilities standard of proof "has been applied to the great majority of categories of claims in international arbitration"). *See also, e.g.*, *Tokios Tokelės v. Ukraine*, ICSID Case No. ARB/02/18, Award dated July 26, 2007 ("*Tokios Tokelės v. Ukraine*") ¶ 124 (observing that "the usual standard ... requires the party making an assertion to persuade the decision-maker that it is more likely than not to be true"); *Ioannis Kardassopoulos and Ron*

fraud, corruption, or other serious illegality, most courts and tribunals have applied a higher standard of proof.[115] Thus, the Iran-U.S. Claims Tribunal holds that allegations of forgery or fraud "must be proved with a higher degree of probability than other allegations," and that "[t]he minimum quantum of evidence that will be required to satisfy the Tribunal may be described as 'clear and convincing evidence,' although the Tribunal deems that precise terminology less important than the enhanced proof requirement that it expresses."[116] The Court of Arbitration for Sport ("CAS") likewise applies a higher standard of "comfortable satisfaction" to allegations of corruption, price-fixing, and doping, in view of "the nature of the conduct in question and the paramount importance of fighting corruption of any kind in sport and also considering the restricted powers of the investigative authorities of the governing bodies of sport…."[117]

Applying this higher standard, CAS panels have rejected allegations of corruption as unproven even where the evidence established that the allegations were likely true. In one such case, the Fédération Internationale de Football Association ("FIFA") had banned Mr. Mohammad Bin Hammam for allegedly bribing delegates of the Caribbean Football Union ("CFU") to support his candidacy for FIFA president. As the CAS panel hearing Mr. Bin Hammam's appeal explained, it was undisputed that Mr. Bin Hammam made a speech about his candidacy at a CFU meeting, and that after he left the room, FIFA's vice president, Jack Warner, invited each CFU delegate to collect a "gift" in the boardroom consisting of an unmarked envelope with US$ 40,000 in cash.[118] The CAS panel found "it to be more likely than not that Mr. Bin Hammam was the source of the money," and that he "gave the money, assuming him to be the source, to

*Fuchs v. The Republic of Georgia*, ICSID Cases Nos. ARB/05/18 and ARB/07/15, Award dated Mar. 3, 2010 ¶ 229 (finding that "the principle articulated by the vast majority of arbitral tribunals" is to apply "a balance of probabilities" standard of proof).

115 *See, e.g.*, O'Malley, Rules of Evidence at 208–212; Gary Born, International Commercial Arbitration (2d ed., 2014) § 15.09 (commenting that "allegations of wrongdoing, particularly serious wrongdoing such as criminal acts, fraud, corruption, and the like, require more convincing evidence than other facts," which in his view is "sensible" "both in evidentiary terms and in discouraging baseless allegations of misconduct").

116 *Dadras Int'l Islamic Republic of Iran*, Iran-U.S. Claims Tribunal, Award dated Nov. 7, 1995, Iran-U.S. Claims Tribunal Reports, 31 (2001) at 127, 162.

117 *FK Pobeda et al. v. UEFA*, CAS 2009/A/1920 ¶ 26. *See also, e.g., Oriekhov v. UEFA*, CAS 2010/A/2172 ¶¶ 20, 53; *Bin Hammam v. Fédération Internationale de Football Association*, CAS 2011/A/2625, Award dated July 19, 2012 ("*Bin Hammam v. FIFA*") ¶¶ 36–39; *Olympiakos Volou FC v. UEFA*, CAS 2011/A/2528, ¶ 134; *FC Metalist et. al. v. FFU*, CAS 2010/A/2267 ¶ 732; Dr. Chris Davies, *The 'Comfortable Satisfaction Standard of Proof: Applied by the Court of Arbitration For Sport in Drug-Related Cases*, UNDALR (2002).

118 *Bin Hammam v. FIFA* ¶ 49.

Mr. Warner."[119] A majority of the panel, however, was "not convinced to the standard of 'comfortable satisfaction' that Mr. Bin Hammam made monies available to delegates attending the CFU meeting ... for the purposes of inducing them to vote for him" in the FIFA election.[120] Thus, while "not making any sort of affirmative finding of innocence in relation to Mr. Bin Hammam," the majority concluded that the evidence was insufficient "to reach the standard of comfortable satisfaction in relation to the matters on which [he] was charged," and that it therefore was "a situation of '*case not proven*'."[121]

Tribunals in numerous investment arbitrations similarly have applied a higher standard of proof to allegations of corruption, fraud, and similar illegality. For example:

- The ICSID tribunal in *Rumeli v. Kazakhstan* held that the claimants' allegation of a conspiracy to benefit the president of Kazakhstan and his family "must, if it is to be supported only by circumstantial evidence, be proved by evidence which leads clearly and convincingly to the inference that a conspiracy has occurred."[122]
- The ICSID tribunal in *Siag v. Egypt* held that Egypt's allegations of forgery would have to meet "the American standard of 'clear and convincing evidence,' that being somewhere between the traditional civil standard of 'preponderance of the evidence' (otherwise known as the 'balance of probabilities'), and the criminal standard of 'beyond reasonable doubt.'" The tribunal further remarked: "It is common in most legal systems for serious allegations such as fraud to be held to a high standard of proof. The same is the case in international proceedings...."[123]

119 *Id.* ¶¶ 85–87.

120 *Id.* ¶ 96. *See also id.* ¶ 88 (finding that "other scenarios" besides bribery were plausible, including that "Mr. Bin Hammam gave the money to Mr. Warner as a token of appreciation for setting up the meeting, or perhaps for some assistance given in the past on another matter"). The dissenting arbitrator's opinion in that case is not public.

121 *Id.* ¶ 95 (seeking "to make clear that this conclusion should not be taken to diminish the significance of its finding that it is more likely than not that Mr. Bin Hammam was the source of the monies that were brought into Trinidad and Tobago and eventually distributed at the meeting by Mr. Warner") (emphasis in original). *See also, e.g., Arnaud Di Benedetto v. FIT*, CAS 2014/A/3519 & *Bastien Cotte-Barrot v. FIT*, CAS 2014/A/3520 ¶ 84 (sole arbitrator "not comfortably satisfied that Stefano Emmi's nose was broken by a punch in the nose—even if it might appear 'more likely than not'").

122 *Rumeli Telekom A.S. and Telsim Mobil Telekomunikasyon Hizmetleir A.S. v. Republic of Kazakhstan*, ICSID Case No. ARB/05/16, Award dated July 29, 2008 ("*Rumeli v. Kazakhstan*") ¶ 709 (noting that such allegations must be assessed "with particular care"). *See also Oostergetel v. Slovak Republic* ¶ 303 fn. 149 (quoting same).

123 *Siag v. Egypt* ¶¶ 325–326; *id.* at fn. 389 (observing that an "alternative term with the same meaning is that employed in CAS anti-doping arbitrations, namely proof to the 'comfortable satisfaction' of the Tribunal").

- The ICSID tribunal in *Bayindir v. Pakistan* held that Bayindir's evidence of an alleged conspiracy would have "to exclude any reasonable doubt," and that "the standard for proving bad faith is a demanding one, in particular if bad faith is to be established on the basis of circumstantial evidence."[124]
- The ICSID tribunal in *EDF v. Romania* held that "[t]he seriousness of the accusation of corruption in the present case, considering that it involves officials at the highest level of the Romanian Government at the time, demands clear and convincing evidence," and that "[t]here is general consensus among international tribunals and commentators regarding the need for a high standard of proof of corruption."[125]
- The ICSID tribunal in *Liman v. Kazakhstan* held that the claimants had "to *prove* corruption" and that it was "not sufficient to present evidence which could possibly indicate that there might have been or even probably was corruption." The tribunal further observed that, although "it is very difficult to prove corruption because secrecy is inherent in such cases," "corruption is a serious allegation" and "both Parties agree that the standard of proof in this respect is a high one."[126]
- The ICSID tribunal in *Saba Fakes v. Turkey* held that "the burden of proof of any allegations of impropriety is particularly heavy."[127]
- The ICSID tribunal in *H&H v. Egypt* held that "corruption allegations are a very serious matter, particularly against government officials, as they involve criminal conduct and therefore cannot be taken lightly. By the same token, because of the gravity of such allegations, the evidentiary threshold must be high."[128]
- The ICSID tribunal in the resubmitted *Fraport v. Philippines* arbitration held that, "in view of the consequences of corruption on the investor's ability to claim the BIT [bilateral investment treaty] protection, evidence must be clear and convincing so as to reasonably make-believe that the facts, as alleged, have occurred."[129]

---

124 *Bayindir Insaat Turizm Ve Sanayi A.S. v. Islamic Republic of Pakistan*, ICSID Case No. ARB/03/29, Award dated Aug. 27, 2009 ¶¶ 142–143 (further noting that, in the *Corfu Channel* case, the ICJ "expressly held that 'proof may be drawn from inferences of fact, provided they leave *no room* for reasonable doubt'").

125 *EDF v. Romania* ¶ 221.

126 *Liman v. Kazakhstan* ¶¶ 422–424.

127 *Mr. Saba Fakes v. Republic of Turkey*, ICSID Case No. ARB/07/20, Award dated July 14, 2010 ("*Saba Fakes v. Turkey*") ¶ 131.

128 *H&H Enterprises Investments, Inc. v. Arab Republic of Egypt*, ICSID Case No. ARB/09/15, Excerpts of Award dated May 6, 2014 ("*H&H v. Egypt*") ¶ 390.

129 *Fraport v. Philippines II* ¶ 479.

– The ICSID tribunal in *Karkey v. Pakistan* held that "the seriousness of the accusation of corruption in the present case, including the fact that it involves officials at the highest level of the Pakistani Government at the time, requires clear and convincing evidence. There is indeed a large consensus among international tribunals regarding the need for a high standard of proof of corruption."[130]

Other tribunals in investment arbitrations have taken a slightly different approach. The ICSID tribunal in *Libananco v. Turkey*, for example, observed that "fraud is a serious allegation," but did "not consider that this (without more) requires it to apply a heightened standard of proof."[131] Rather, while affirming that "the graver the charge, the more confidence there must be in the evidence relied on," the *Libananco* tribunal concluded that "this does not necessarily entail a higher standard of proof. It may simply require more persuasive evidence, in the case of a fact that is inherently improbable, in order for the Tribunal to be satisfied that the burden of proof has been discharged."[132]

The ICSID tribunal in *Rompetrol v. Romania* likewise declined to apply the U.S. standard of clear and convincing evidence, observing that its powers to assess the evidence freely under the ICSID arbitration rules weighed heavily against any argument that it was "bound in advance to expect or to require specific levels of proof or of rebuttal in respect of particular factual allegations."[133] The *Rompetrol* tribunal, however, distinguished the misconduct alleged in that case from more serious allegations of bad faith, fraud, or corruption, which were not raised, and observed that "there may well be situations in which, given the nature of an allegation of wrongful (in the wildest sense) conduct, and in the light of the position of the person concerned, an adjudicator would be reluctant to find the allegation proved in the absence of a sufficient weight of positive evidence—as opposed to pure probabilities or circumstantial inferences."[134] It therefore is uncertain what standard of proof the tribunal would have applied to allegations of corruption. Moreover, while the *Rompetrol* applied "the normal rule of the 'balance of probabilities'" to most of the factual issues raised, it decided to "adopt a more nuanced approach" where necessary and to determine "in each discrete instance whether an allegation of seriously

130 *Karkey v. Pakistan* ¶ 492.

131 *Libananco Holdings Co. Ltd. v. Republic of Turkey*, ICSID Case No. ARB/06/8, Award dated Sept. 2, 2011 ¶ 125.

132 *Id.* ¶ 125. *See also id.* ¶ 126 (noting that the issue of the standard of proof was "of academic interest only" and was "not dispositive in these proceedings").

133 *Rompetrol v. Romania* ¶¶ 180, 182 (quoting the *Libananco* award with approval).

134 *Id.* ¶ 182 (noting that "the particular circumstances would be determinative, and in the Tribunal's view defy codification").

wrongful conduct by a Romanian state official at either the administrative or policymaking level has been proved on the basis of the entire body of direct and indirect evidence before it."[135]

Thus, while the *Libananco* and *Rompetrol* tribunals both applied the ordinary standard of a preponderance of evidence to the allegations of wrongdoing raised in those cases, their observations are consistent with the majority view that a more rigorous assessment and more compelling evidence are required to find fraud or corruption.

Accordingly, in *ECE Projektmanagement v. Czech Republic*, an investment arbitration administered by the PCA under the UNCITRAL arbitration rules, the tribunal took note of the different views expressed by tribunals with regard to the applicable standard of proof, including in *Libananco*, and concluded that, irrespective of the standard applied, the tribunal "must examine with care the facts alleged to prove corruption."[136] The *ECE Projektmanagement* tribunal also acknowledged that "acts of corruption are rarely admitted or documented" and thus are difficult to prove.[137] Nonetheless, the tribunal observed that corruption allegations "are very serious indeed," and that a tribunal therefore "must weigh the evidence with care, both to see whether the allegation is made out ... and at the same time to safeguard those against whom corruption is alleged, if the allegations turn out to be unproven."[138]

Very few tribunals have disagreed with that view. One such decision, *Tokios Tokelės v. Ukraine*, is now 12 years old and precedes all of the decisions described above. In that case, Tokios Tokelės alleged that Ukrainian agencies and officials including prosecutors and courts had carried out a coordinated and unlawful conspiracy (*nayizd*) to damage its business in order to punish the company for supporting the opposition politician Yulia Tymoshenko.[139] The *Tokios Tokelės* tribunal found "serious logical problems" with requiring "proof of more than the balance of probabilities where an allegation of gross misconduct is made against a highly placed person."[140] The tribunal concluded that

---

135 *Id.* ¶ 183.

136 *ECE Projektmanagement International GmbH and Kommanditgesellschaft PANTA Achtundsechzigste Grundstücksgesellschaft mbH & Co v. Czech Republic*, PCA Case No. 2010-5, Award dated Sept. 19, 2013 ("*ECE Projektmanagement v. Czech Republic*") ¶ 4.873 (citing *Libananco* as an example where a tribunal "found that the seriousness of the allegation does not necessarily mean that the tribunal must apply a heightened standard of proof").

137 *Id.* ¶ 4.876.

138 *Id.* ¶¶ 4.872, 4.876.

139 *Tokios Tokelės v. Ukraine* ¶ 12.

140 *Id.* ¶ 124. Conversely, the tribunal observed that lowering the standard of proof on the ground that a conspiracy would be difficult to prove was untenable "for its consequence

evidentiary requirements could not be "heightened purely on the grounds of deference or comity or otherwise," and that "if it is said that this is an example of the common-sense principle that an inherently unlikely allegation requires stronger than usual supporting evidence before it is accepted, contemporary experience shows how unrealistic it can be to assume that important persons will not behave badly."[141] The tribunal therefore refused to make any such assumptions one way or the other, and held that Tokios Tokelės must prove that the alleged existence and causal relevance of a *nayizd* was "more likely than not to be true."[142]

More recently, in *Union Fenosa v. Egypt*, the ICSID tribunal held that the standard of proof for allegations of corruption "remains 'the balance of probabilities'" and that "[t]here is no reason in this arbitration, which is not a criminal proceeding, to impose a higher standard of proof."[143] While it relied on the *Libananco* decision for this conclusion, the *Union Fenosa* tribunal did not address the *Libananco* tribunal's observations that graver charges require more confidence in the evidence and that allegations of illegality therefore may require more persuasive evidence.

Similarly, the tribunal in *Chevron v. Ecuador* applied the "balance of probabilities" standard of proof to allegations of judicial corruption, although it did not explain its reasons for applying this standard.[144] Thus, while several decisions support applying the ordinary standard of proof to allegations of corruption and fraud, this appears to be a minority view. In most cases, as set forth above, tribunals will either impose a higher standard of proof or will exercise great care and require more compelling evidence to prove that allegations of corruption and fraud are likely true.

### 4.3 *Corruption May Be Proved through Circumstantial (Rather than Direct) Evidence*

As to the type of evidence required to prove corruption, Bin Cheng explains that, in cases where direct evidence of a fact is not available, "it is a general

is that the person who makes the allegation may be entitled to succeed even if it is less likely than not that the allegation is true." *Id.*

141 *Id.*

142 *Id.*

143 *Union Fenosa v. Egypt* ¶ 7.52.

144 *Chevron Corp. and Texaco Petroleum Co. v. The Republic of Ecuador*, PCA Case No. 2009-2003, UNCITRAL, Second Partial Award on Track II dated Aug. 30, 2018 ("*Chevron v. Ecuador*") ¶ 8.42 (holding that "the balance of probabilities remains the standard of proof, with the claimant bearing the overall legal burden of proof"); *id.* ¶¶ 5.230, 6.107, 6.110.

principle of law that proof may be administered by means of circumstantial evidence."[145]

Circumstantial evidence is common to all legal systems, including in criminal cases requiring proof beyond a reasonable doubt.[146] As the ICJ observed in the *Corfu Channel* case, "indirect evidence is admitted in all systems of law, and its use is recognized by international decisions. It must be regarded as of special weight when it is based on a series of facts linked together and leading logically to a single conclusion."[147] Consistent with the majority view on this issue, Judge Azevedo further observed in his dissenting opinion in that case:

> A condemnation, even to the death penalty, may be well-founded on indirect evidence and may nevertheless have the same value as a judgment by a court which has founded its conviction on the evidence of witnesses. It would be going too far for an international court to insist on direct and visual evidence and to refuse to admit, after reflection, a reasonable amount of human presumptions with a view to reaching that state of moral, human certainty with which, despite the risks of occasional errors, a court of justice must be content.[148]

Numerous tribunals likewise have held that corruption and other illegal acts may be proven through circumstantial evidence. Thus, for example, in investment arbitration:

- The ICSID tribunal in *Tokios Tokelės v. Ukraine* stated: "Certainly, any sensible tribunal considering an allegation of this kind will recognize that the need to rely on circumstantial or secondary evidence does not necessarily

145 Cheng, General Principles of Law at 322.

146 *See, e.g., R. v. Taylor* (1928) 21 cr. App R 20; *United States v. Johns*, 26 Fed Cas. 616 No. 15481, C.C. Pa. 1806; *State v. Butler*, 94 N.E. 457 (1949); *Commonwealth v. Wentzel*, 61 A.2d 309 (1948). *See also Sufficiency of Circumstantial Evidence in a Criminal Case*, 55 COL. L. REV. 549, 549 (1955).

147 *United Kingdom of Great Britain and Northern Ireland v. Albania (Corfu Channel)*, ICJ, Judgment dated Apr. 9, 1949 ("*Corfu Channel*") at 18 (further observing that "proof may be drawn from inferences of fact, provided that they leave no room for reasonable doubt"); *but see* Sowed Juma Mayanja, "Circumstantial Evidence and Its Admissibility in Criminal Proceedings: A Comparative Analysis of the Common Law and Islamic Law Systems," 67 J.L. POL'Y & GLOBALIZATION 26, 31 (2017) (discussing the three differing views of Muslim jurists on convicting a person based on circumstantial evidence under Islamic law).

148 *Corfu Channel*, Dissenting Opinion of Judge Azevedo at 90–91.

tell against it, but this does not dispense with the need for evidence of one kind or another sufficient to take the proof over the barrier."[149]

- The ICSID tribunal in *Rumeli v. Kazakhstan* observed that the claimants' evidence of a conspiracy was "mainly, if not wholly circumstantial, but it is in the nature of such an allegation that direct evidence of a conspiracy is unlikely to be available."[150]
- The tribunal in *Oostergetel v. Slovakia*, an ad hoc proceeding under the UNCITRAL arbitration rules, commented that, "[f]or obvious reasons, it is generally difficult to bring positive proof of corruption. Yet, corruption can also be proven by circumstantial evidence."[151]
- The ICSID tribunal in *Metal-Tech v. Uzbekistan* observed that "corruption is by essence difficult to establish and that it is thus generally admitted that it can be shown through circumstantial evidence."[152]
- The ICSID tribunal in *Union Fenosa v. Egypt* remarked: "As has long been recognized, corruption is rarely proven by direct cogent evidence; but, rather, it usually depends upon an accumulation of circumstantial evidence. Circumstantial evidence of corruption is as good as direct evidence in proving corruption."[153]

Regardless of the applicable standard of proof, it therefore is evident that corruption may be proved through circumstantial evidence. Such circumstantial evidence, however, must establish the specific facts alleged. Thus, the tribunal in *ECE Projektmanagement* observed that corruption allegations must be supported by "either some direct evidence or compelling circumstantial evidence," and that the "mere existence of suspicions cannot, in the absence of sufficiently firm corroborative evidence, be equated with proof."[154] The tribunal accordingly concluded that "blanket condemnatory allegations which can have the appearance of an attempt to 'poison the well'" are insufficient to prove corruption:

> The Tribunal must begin by stating that it finds to be deeply unattractive an argument to the effect that 'everyone knows that the [State] is corrupt; therefore, there was corruption in this case …' … References to other instances of alleged corruption may prove that corruption exists in the State, but it does little to advance the argument that corruption existed

149 *Tokios Tokeles v. Ukraine* ¶ 124.
150 *Rumeli v. Kazakhstan* ¶ 709.
151 *Oostergetel v. Slovak Republic* ¶ 303.
152 *Metal-Tech v. Uzbekistan* ¶ 243.
153 *Union Fenosa v. Egypt* ¶ 7.52.
154 *ECE Projektmanagement v. Czech Republic* ¶ 4.876.

> in the specific events giving rise to the claim. Nor do allegations of this kind, however seriously advanced, give rise to a burden on the [responding party] to 'disprove' the existence of corruption. While the present Tribunal is therefore willing to 'connect the dots', if that is appropriate, the dots have to exist and they must be substantiated by relevant and probative evidence relating to the specific allegations made in the case before it.[155]

Other tribunals likewise have held that generalized allegations of corruption lack probative value.[156] Accordingly, while corruption may be proved through circumstantial evidence by "connecting the dots," it is not sufficient to allege generally that an entire government or judiciary is corrupt, or that a person or entity acted corruptly in another context.

### 4.4 *Tribunals Have the Power to Draw Adverse Inferences against Either Party for Failing to Produce Evidence*

Closely related to the issue of circumstantial evidence is the power of tribunals to draw adverse inferences if either party fails to produce evidence.

One of the earliest and most famous examples of a court drawing an adverse inference was the English case of *Armory v. Delamirie* in the early 1700s. In that case, a chimney sweep's boy found a jewel in the setting of a ring and brought it to a goldsmith to be valued. The goldsmith's apprentice stole the jewel. The court found the goldsmith responsible for his apprentice's actions and held that he was liable for the lost value of the jewel. In assessing damages, the court instructed the jury that, "unless the defendant did produce the jewel, and shew it not to be of the finest water, they should presume the strongest against him, and make the value of the best jewels the measure of their damages: which they accordingly did."[157]

Many domestic laws and arbitration acts now authorize courts and tribunals to draw this type of adverse inference against either party for failing to produce evidence.[158] ICSID Arbitration Rule 34(3) similarly provides: "The

155 *Id.* ¶ 4.879. *See also id.* ¶ 4.885 ("Although a company may have been convicted of criminal offences in other contexts, it does not follow that it has engaged in criminal or improper activity in the events giving rise to the claim.").

156 *See, e.g., Liman v. Kazakhstan* ¶ 422 (holding that "generalized allegations of corruption in the Republic of Kazakhstan do not meet Claimants' burden of proof").

157 Alexander Sevan Bedrosyan, "Adverse Inferences in International Arbitration," 38 U. PA. J. INT'L LAW 241 at 252–253 (citing (1722) 93 Eng. Rep. 664 (K.B.)).

158 *See, e.g.*, English Arbitration Act of 1996, c. 23, § 41(7)(b) ("If a party fails to comply with any other kind of peremptory order ... the tribunal may ... draw such adverse inferences

parties shall cooperate with the Tribunal in the production of the evidence and in the other measures provided for.... The Tribunal shall take formal note of the failure of a party to comply with its obligation under this paragraph and of any reasons given for such failure."[159] ICSID tribunals thus are expressly empowered to draw adverse inferences against either party for failing to comply with their obligations to produce evidence.[160]

It also is widely recognized that arbitral tribunals have the power to draw adverse inferences even if the applicable arbitral rules do not address the issue.[161] For example, while the UNCITRAL arbitration rules are silent with regard to adverse inferences, the UNCITRAL notes on organizing arbitral proceedings confirm that, "if the requested party duly invited to produce documentary evidence fails to do so within the established period of time, without showing sufficient cause for such failure, the arbitral tribunal is free to draw its conclusions from the failure and may make the award on the evidence before it."[162]

In addition, the IBA Rules on the Taking of Evidence frequently are used as guidelines in international proceedings. Article 9(5) of the IBA Rules provides:

---

from the act of non-compliance as the circumstances justify."); Australia Commercial Arbitration Act 2017, Part 5, Section 26(3)(b) ("If a party fails to comply with a peremptory order, the arbitral tribunal may ... draw such adverse inferences from the failure to comply as the circumstances justify."); Geneva Code of Civil Procedure, Art. 186(2) ("Le juge peut ordonner à la partie qui détient une pièce utile à la solution du litige de la produire, même si le fardeau de la preuve ne lui incombe pas. En cas de refus sans motif légitime, le fait allégué par la partie adverse peut être tenu pour avéré.") (Translation: "The judge can order a party holding a document which is relevant for the resolution of the dispute to produce it, even if that party does not have the burden of proof. If the party refuses without legitimate reason, the fact alleged by the other party may be considered established.").

159 ICSID Arbitration Rule 34(2) provides that the Tribunal may, if it deems it necessary at any stage of the proceeding, call upon the parties to produce documents, witnesses, and experts, and visit any place connected with the dispute or conduct inquiries there. *See also* ICSID Convention Art. 43.

160 *See, e.g., Rumeli v. Kazakhstan* ¶ 444 ("If a party does not comply with its obligations, for instance by refusing to produce the requested documents and witnesses, the Arbitral Tribunal is authorized to draw adverse conclusions from the party's behavior."); *Waste Management v. Mexico*, ICSID Case No. ARB(AF)/00/3, Procedural Order Concerning Disclosure of Documents dated Oct. 1, 2002 ¶ 6 (observing that "[t]he ultimate sanction for non-disclosure is the drawing of an adverse inference").

161 van Houtte, Adverse Inferences at 199 (observing that "[i]t is widely accepted that arbitral tribunals are allowed to draw adverse inferences, even if most arbitration rules ... do not provide any explicit provision to that effect").

162 UNCITRAL Notes on Organizing Arbitral Proceedings ¶ 51. *See also* UNCITRAL Arbitration Rules, Art. 30(3) ("If a party, duly invited by the arbitral tribunal to produce documents, exhibits or other evidence, fails to do so within the established period of time, without showing sufficient cause for such failure, the arbitral tribunal may make the award on the evidence before it.").

"If a Party fails without satisfactory explanation to produce any Document requested in a Request to Produce to which it has not objected in due time or fails to produce any Document ordered to be produced by the Arbitral Tribunal, the Arbitral Tribunal may infer that such document would be adverse to the interests of that Party." Thus, regardless of the applicable arbitral rules, Durward Sandifer states that "the most effective sanction" to deter a party from concealing evidence "is the threat to draw an adverse inference against the party in the event of continued refusal to bring forward the needed documents."[163]

As the IBA rules reflect, an adverse inference may only be drawn against a party for failing to produce evidence if that party has possession, custody, or control of the evidence and was ordered to produce it.[164] In order to ensure due process and the right of defense of both parties, the tribunal also must allow the party to explain its failure to produce the evidence and take into account the reasons provided, with the consequence that an adverse inference may not be drawn if the party has a valid objection to producing it.[165] Further, based on the evidence in the record, the tribunal must be convinced that the missing evidence would prove the inference requested and could not instead support some other explanation.[166]

If these requirements are met and due process is ensured, the tribunal may draw an adverse inference that may have a decisive impact, even in cases involving alleged fraud and corruption.[167] For example, in *Europe Cement v.*

163 Durward V. Sandifer, EVIDENCE BEFORE INTERNATIONAL TRIBUNALS 147 (1975). *See also* O'Malley, Rules of Evidence at 216 (explaining that "parties come to the procedure in international arbitration with the obligation to cooperate with the tribunal's efforts to establish the facts of the case," that "[r]efusing to produce evidence that has been called for by the arbitrator is naturally a breach of that duty," and, therefore, "[t]hat a party may suffer an inference drawn against it because of its non-observance of the duty to cooperate is a widely accepted result").

164 van Houtte, Adverse Inferences, at 201–202.

165 *Id.* at 202–203, 208–209, 214.

166 *Id.* at 207 (observing that the inference must be consistent with the facts in the record and have a logical relation to the likely nature of the missing evidence, and that "if many different inferences can be drawn from the non-production (or non-availability) of some evidence, the relation between that missing evidence and the inference may not be strong enough to justify the inference").

167 *Id.* at 202 (noting that adverse inferences may "have a determining impact on the decision"). *See also, e.g., Doe and another v. Skegg and another*, EWHC 3746 (2006) (Ch) ¶ 36 (holding that proving fraud is "notoriously one of the most difficult things to prove in civil proceedings," and that "it is also the case that in most fraud cases, a conclusion reached by the court that fraudulent conduct has taken place, will be based upon inference rather than by direct evidence").

*Turkey*, an ICSID additional facility arbitration, Turkey contested the authenticity of the copies of share certificates submitted by Europe Cement for purposes of establishing its ownership of its alleged investment. In view of certain irregularities noted in the copies of those share certificates, the tribunal ordered Europe Cement to produce the originals, which it refused to do.[168] The tribunal therefore drew the "strong inference" that the original share certificates "were not produced either because Europe Cement did not have them or because they would not withstand forensic scrutiny."[169] Based on that inference, the tribunal concluded that it did not have jurisdiction and that the claim was founded "on an assertion of ownership which the evidence suggests was fraudulent."[170]

A tribunal's finding of fraud or corruption based on an adverse inference does not mean it shifted the burden of proof. As Vera van Houtte explains in her publication on adverse inferences in international arbitration, the two issues are distinct and should not be conflated:

> The obligation of the opposite party to cooperate in the production of evidence, even if it follows from the general principle of good faith ... does not concern the burden of proof and does not cause its shifting. It is within the context of the assessment of the evidence that the judge decides about the result of the cooperation of the opposite party or that he draws consequences from a refusal to cooperate in relation to the bringing of evidence.[171]

As Ms. van Houtte further explains, while an adverse inference may be part of the tribunal's overall assessment of the evidence, an adverse inference by itself "is insufficient evidence to justify an *intime conviction* or to create a 'preponderance of evidence.'"[172] The party bearing the burden of proof therefore must support its case with actual evidence and "cannot possibly win its case on the basis of adverse inference alone."[173]

168 *Europe Cement Investment & Trade S.A. v. Republic of Turkey*, ICSID Case No. ARB(AF)/07/2, Award dated Aug. 13, 2009 ¶¶ 99–103.

169 *Id.* ¶ 152.

170 *Id.* ¶¶ 2, 170, 185 (dismissing the claim in its entirety and further observing that "the evidence on this case points to the conclusion that the Claimant did not own shares in [its alleged investment] at the relevant date").

171 van Houtte, Adverse Inferences at 196.

172 *Id.* at 198.

173 *Id.* at 206 ("An award must be justified by evidence and arguments brought by the winning party. An adverse inference is only one element among many that make up the total body of evidence that enables the tribunal to reach a decision.").

Having set out the applicable rules of evidence above, we analyze below how corruption has been proven in practice in investment arbitration.

## V From Theory to Practice: Proving Corruption in Investment Arbitration

Parties have succeeded in proving corruption in only a few investment arbitrations. Several of these cases turned on damning admissions made by the party found to have paid bribes.

The first and most infamous of these cases was *World Duty Free v. Kenya*, an ICSID arbitration that arose under a contract to build, maintain, and operate duty-free complexes at the Nairobi and Mombassa airports. In that case, World Duty Free's chairman, Mr. Nasir Ibrahim Ali, admitted paying a "personal donation" to the President of Kenya, Mr. Daniel arap Moi, as "part of the consideration … to obtain the contract."[174]

Specifically, in a witness statement submitted with World Duty Free's memorial, Mr. Ali stated that he remitted a US$ 2 million letter of credit to Mr. Rashid Sajjad, who "was politically and powerfully connected in the Kenyan Government" and was "very close" to President Moi, and that Mr. Sajjad then accompanied him to a meeting at President Moi's personal residence.[175] Mr. Ali further explained that, upon arriving at the meeting, Mr. Sajjad delivered a briefcase filled with US$ 500,000 in cash that he had drawn from Mr. Ali's letter of credit, and that, after the meeting, the briefcase was returned to them filled with fresh corn:

> I understood that Sajjad had received the cash worth US$500,000 against the letter of credit on 16 February 1989. He had then arranged for this to be exchanged into Kenyan Shillings (KSh). He brought the KSh in cash to my meeting with HEDAM [His Excellency Daniel arap Moi] in a brown briefcase. When we entered the room where the President received us, he put the briefcase by the wall and left it there. After the meeting we collected the briefcase from where we had left it. On the departing journey I looked in the briefcase and saw that the money had been replaced with fresh corn.
>
> I felt uncomfortable with the idea of handing over this 'personal donation' which appeared to me to be a bribe. However, this was the President,

174 *World Duty Free v. Kenya* ¶¶ 66, 130.

175 *Id.* ¶ 130.

> and I was given to understand that it was lawful and that I didn't have a choice if I wanted the investment contract. I paid the money ... treating it as part of the consideration for the agreement and documented it fully....[176]

At the hearing held in that case, Mr. Ali confirmed his written testimony and added that Mr. Sajjad had explained to him that the fresh corn in the briefcase meant "the President likes your proposal; it is a very good sign."[177]

It is axiomatic that neither party has any obligation to prove facts admitted by the opposing party.[178] Based on Mr. Ali's admissions and the fact that Kenya did not deny the payment to President Moi in the circumstances he described, the *World Duty Free* tribunal found that the payment "must then be considered as established."[179] While World Duty Free denied that the payment was a bribe and contended that it was a lawful "gift of protocol" made for a public purpose according to Kenya's cultural practice of "Harambee,"[180] the tribunal found that the payment was not made for a public purpose but instead was paid to obtain an audience with the President and "above all to obtain during that audience the agreement of the President on the contemplated investment."[181] The tribunal therefore concluded that the payment was a bribe to obtain the contract on which World Duty Free's claims were founded.[182] The tribunal further observed that "this is not a case which turns on legal presumptions, statutory deeming provisions or different standards of proof" under the laws applicable to that proceeding.[183] Rather, the tribunal emphasized that its finding of bribery was "indisputable on the evidence adduced," and that "the decisive evidential materials came from [World Duty Free] itself, including Mr. Ali's own written and oral testimony."[184]

---

176 *Id.*

177 *Id.* ¶ 131.

178 *See, e.g.*, Cheng, General Principles of Law at 307 ("Allegations of the parties of the truth of which the tribunal does not take judicial notice or which are not presumed by it, have to be proved, unless they are admitted by the other party.").

179 *World Duty Free v. Kenya* ¶ 132.

180 *Id.* ¶¶ 110, 120, 133.

181 *Id.* ¶ 136.

182 *Id. See also id.* ¶ 167 (finding that "Mr. Ali paid a substantial bribe in cash, in Kenyan schillings, to the Kenyan head of state in March 1989," that this "bribe was made covertly" and was "an intrinsic part of the overall transaction, without which no contract would have been concluded between the parties: Mr. Ali himself regarded the payment as part of the contractual consideration paid," and that "Mr. Ali made the payment to the Kenyan President intending to induce the President to act in his principal's favour" and "he also intended that bribe to remain confidential").

183 *Id.* ¶ 166.

184 *Id.*

In the aftermath of that decision, Kenya's legal counsel, Constantin Partasides, commented that Mr. Ali's testimony was "quite extraordinary" and that the tribunal's finding of bribery was "destined to remain an unusual decision because of the particular circumstances in which it was rendered."[185] He asked rhetorically, "How often can we expect a claimant itself to offer the evidence of illegality that will—in all likelihood—consign its claim to failure?"[186]

Yet, just a year after Mr. Partasides made those comments, another party representative proffered similar ill-fated testimony in the ICSID case of *Azpetrol v. Azerbaijan*. As the tribunal in *Azpetrol* recounted, Mr. Peter Booster, a director of the several claimant companies in that case, testified during cross-examination at the hearing "that he had provided funds to bribe officials in Azerbaijan in early 2006."[187] One day after Mr. Booster testified, the parties jointly applied to adjourn the proceedings, which the tribunal agreed to do.[188] Azerbaijan then formally requested the dismissal of the proceedings on grounds of corruption.[189]

In an unsuccessful attempt to salvage his companies' claims, Mr. Booster thereafter filed a letter asserting that his testimony about bribing officials in Azerbaijan "had been untrue and that he wished to retract it."[190] Ultimately, while the tribunal expressed doubt about the veracity of Mr. Booster's retraction, it did not take any action in respect of his letter or make any findings regarding the bribery allegations because, before it could do so, the parties agreed to settle and discontinue the case without any payment by either side.[191] Thus, while the *Azpetrol* case did not technically result in a finding of corruption, it is evident from the record that Mr. Booster's admissions motivated the claimants to withdraw their claims.[192]

185 Chatham House International Law Discussion Group Meeting, Mar. 28, 2007: "World Duty Free v. The Republic of Kenya: A Unique Precedent?" at 2–3, 7.

186 *Id.* at 7.

187 *Azpetrol International Holdings B.V., Azpetrol Group B.V., and Azpetrol Oil Services Group B.V. v. Republic of Azerbaijan*, ICSID Case No. ARB/06/15, Award dated Sept. 8, 2009 ¶ 6 (explaining that Mr. Booster's "evidence was that these bribes were paid in order to protect unnamed individuals in Azerbaijan").

188 *Id.* ¶ 6.

189 *Id.* ¶ 7.

190 *Id.* ¶ 17 fn. 3.

191 *Id.* ¶ 17 fn. 3 (stating that the tribunal wished "to make clear" that Mr. Booster's letter "does not amount to testimony" as "it was not set out in a witness statement with the normal declaration of truth and Mr. Booster has not been cross-examined upon it," and that the tribunal "had not decided what action, if any, to take regarding the letter when the Settlement Application was made").

192 The claimants subsequently denied that they had concluded a valid settlement agreement and objected to the discontinuance of the proceeding. The tribunal determined,

Similar admissions also were made during the hearing in another ICSID arbitration, *Metal-Tech v. Uzbekistan*. Metal-Tech had obtained the government of Uzbekistan's approval to establish a molybdenum processing joint venture with two State-owned entities.[193] At the hearing, Metal-Tech's chairman and CEO, Mr. Ariel Rosenberg, testified that Metal-Tech had paid approximately US$ 4 million to three alleged consultants who included the brother of the Prime Minister of Uzbekistan and a former government official.[194] Mr. Rosenberg further testified that Metal-Tech's agreements with the consultants predated the establishment of the joint venture, and that the consultants were primarily engaged in "lobbying" activities rather than the services falsely disclosed by Metal-Tech in a public prospectus.[195] The tribunal in *Metal-Tech* emphasized that "[t]hese facts were not alleged by the Respondent; they emerged during the Hearing in the course of the examination of the Claimant's principal witness."[196]

Mr. Rosenberg also testified that the key consultant was Mr. Uygur Sultanov, because "[h]is brother was the Prime Minister at the time, so it really was one of the persons that could facilitate closing red tapes when the [joint venture] was initiated."[197] Moreover, when asked whether he knew that one of the other consultants, Mr. Igor Chijenok, was working in the Office of the President of Uzbekistan when the joint venture was established, Mr. Rosenberg replied: "I know that he was working in a high position in an official position."[198]

In these circumstances, the *Metal-Tech* tribunal observed that, "[a]s in *World Duty Free*," the case did not turn on rules relating to the burden of proof or presumptions, as Metal-Tech itself had proffered testimony that "raised suspicions of corruption" and "required explanations."[199] The tribunal considered that it thus had a duty to inquire about the reasons for the payments admitted by Mr. Rosenberg, and it accordingly issued multiple *ex officio* orders directing Metal-Tech to substantiate its contention that it had paid for legitimate

however, that the parties had settled the dispute and that it thus did not have jurisdiction. *Id.* ¶ 105.

193 *Metal-Tech v. Uzbekistan* ¶¶ 13–18.

194 *Id.* ¶¶ 197–198, 240 (noting that the amount paid was later clarified through financial records as totaling US$ 3.5 million).

195 *Id.* ¶¶ 197–198, 240, 247, 273.

196 *Id.* ¶ 240.

197 *Id.* ¶¶ 226, 350 (further noting Mr. Rosenberg's testimony that "[w]e didn't have any connection to the Government authorities [and] needed somebody that will take us by our hand and show us and pass us all these red tapes, institutes")

198 *Id.* ¶ 225.

199 *Id.* ¶¶ 239, 242–243.

consulting services.[200] Metal-Tech, however, was unable to provide any contemporaneous evidence of any legitimate consulting services, and its excuses for failing to do so were "unconvincing."[201] The tribunal therefore concluded that "the inference that inexorably emerges from this dearth of evidence is that [Metal-Tech] can provide no evidence of services, because no services, or at least no legitimate services at the time of the establishment of [Metal-Tech's] investment, were in fact performed."[202]

The *Metal-Tech* tribunal also found a number of "red flags" of corruption. According to various authorities, common red flags of corruption include, among other things, that a consultant or other intermediary: (i) has a close personal, familial, or professional relationship with a key government decision-maker or their relative; (ii) shows up shortly before government action is to be taken; (iii) claims to know the right people to obtain the desired government action; (iv) lacks experience in the sector; (v) requires "urgent" payments or unusually high commissions; (vi) requests to be paid in cash or through a third person or entity; (vii) provides unspecified services; and (viii) does not reside or have a significant business presence in the country where the project is located.[203] These red flags are not conclusive evidence of corruption, but "are warning signs that need to be taken seriously and investigated."[204] The *Metal-Tech* tribunal accordingly observed that "any adjudicator with good common sense would consider" such red flags "when assessing facts in relation with a

200 *Id.* ¶¶ 241, 246–256.

201 *Id.* ¶¶ 256, 265.

202 *Id.* ¶ 265.

203 *See, e.g.*, FCPA Resource Guide at 22–23; Commentary to OECD Convention on Bribery at 155; ICC International Corporate Integrity Handbook: Fighting Corruption (Fritz Heimann and Francois Vincke, eds., 2008) at 61–62; ICC Commission on Corporate Responsibility and Anti-corruption, *ICC Guidelines on Agents, Intermediaries and Other Third Parties* (2010) at 5–6; Woolf Committee, "Business Ethics, Global Companies and the Defence Industry" (May 2008) at 26. *See also Metal-Tech v. Uzbekistan* ¶ 293 (observing that the various lists of red flags, "although worded differently, have essentially the same content").

204 ICC Commission on Corporate Responsibility and Anti-corruption, *ICC Guidelines on Agents, Intermediaries and Other Third Parties* (2010) at 5 (explaining that "[t]he presence of one or more 'red flags' does not necessarily mean that the transaction cannot go forward, but it does suggest the need for a more in-depth inquiry and the implementation of appropriate compliance safeguards"); FCPA Resource Guide at 24 (stating that, "while certain expenditures are more likely to raise red flags, they will not give rise to prosecution if they are (1) reasonable, (2) bona fide, and (3) directly related to (4) the promotion, demonstration, or explanation of products or services or the execution or performance of a contract").

corruption issue," and that tribunals in several commercial arbitrations had taken such an approach to find corruption.[205]

Based on its assessment of the evidence, the *Metal-Tech* tribunal determined that the payments made to the consultants raised the following red flags of corruption:

- *Amount of payments*: The amount of the payments was "striking," especially in the local context and in comparison with the size of Metal-Tech's alleged investment and the total value of the project.[206]
- *No services or proof of services*: Metal-Tech concluded agreements requiring it to pay the consultants "irrespective of services provided," and, as discussed above, failed to provide any evidence of any legitimate services.[207]
- *Lack of qualification of the consultants*: None of the consultants had any prior experience in the molybdenum industry or possessed any professional qualification to perform the services for which Metal-Tech allegedly retained them.[208]
- *Sham consulting contracts*: Metal-Tech made the payments pursuant to consulting contracts that were not "genuine," but instead "must be deemed a sham designed to conceal the true nature" of the payments to the consultants.[209]
- *Lack of transparency of payee*: The vast majority of the payments were made to shell companies registered in Switzerland and the British Virgin Islands

---

205 *Metal-Tech v. Uzbekistan* ¶ 293 fn. 340. *See also, e.g.*, ICC Case No. 6497 ¶¶ 17–30 (finding that the claimant's commission of 33.33% under Product Agreement Q was "extremely unusual," that the agreement did "not describe the services to be rendered," that the claimant gave "confusing and contradictory testimony" regarding the nature of the services allegedly rendered and provided false explanations for failing to produce witnesses and documents, and that there thus was "a high degree of probability that the real object of Product Agreement Q was to channel bribes to officials in country X"); ICC Case No. 8891, Award of 1998, *Journal du Droit International* 4 (2000) 1076, 1079 ("ICC Case No. 8891") at 1080–1082 (finding that the respondent had agreed to pay a success fee to the claimant to obtain a government contract, that the fee was 18.5% of the contract value which was very high, that the duration of the claimant's activities was very short, that the claimant did not sufficiently explain its activities, and that the true purpose of the payment thus had been to bribe officials to obtain the award of the government contract); ICC Case No. 3916, Award of 1982, *Collection of ICC Arbitral Awards 1974–1985* (Jarvin, Sigvard & Derains, Yves eds. 1990) at 507, 509; ICC Case No. 12990 at 60–61; ICC Case No. 13515, Award dated Apr. 2006, *ICC Bulletin (Supplement)* 24 (2013) ("ICC Case No. 13515") at 66, 71–75.

206 *Metal-Tech v. Uzbekistan* ¶¶ 199–203 (finding that the consulting payments exceeded Metal-Tech's "initial cash contribution to the venture and amounted to nearly 20% of the entire project cost").

207 *Id.* ¶¶ 204–207.

208 *Id.* ¶¶ 208–212.

209 *Id.* ¶¶ 213–218.

that concealed the consultants' ownership interest and were "troubling" for their lack of transparency.[210]

- *Connections with public officials in charge of the investment*: Mr. Sultanov "was the brother of the Prime Minister of Uzbekistan, who had the delegated authority to monitor and oversee [Metal-Tech's] investment," and Mr. Chijenok was "himself a government official" and, indeed, "it was Mr. Chijenok's office that requested Prime Minister Sultanov's opinion on [Metal-Tech's] proposed investment in Uzbekistan."[211]

Metal-Tech also made its final consulting payment in the same month that the President of Uzbekistan dismissed Mr. Sultanov's brother from his then position as Deputy Prime Minister; the alleged State measures underlying Metal-Tech's arbitration claims began almost immediately thereafter.[212] For all of these reasons, the *Metal-Tech* tribunal concluded that the payments made to Messrs. Sultanov and Chijenok were bribes to facilitate the establishment of Metal-Tech's investment in Uzbekistan.[213]

The tribunal in *Spentex v. Uzbekistan* found that Spentex also had made its investment in Uzbekistan through similar bribe payments falsely disguised as consulting fees.[214] The award in *Spentex* is not public, but the tribunal's findings were widely reported in leading arbitration publications. According to those publications, the tribunal found numerous red flags of corruption in connection with millions of dollars paid to a particular consultant on the eve of a public tender, and determined by "connecting the dots" that those payments in fact were bribes to rig the tender and procure the investment.[215]

Finally, the ongoing *Chevron v. Ecuador* case is the rare investment arbitration where the claimants succeeded in proving corruption. The dispute in *Chevron* concerned a judgment of Ecuador's Lago Agrio court ordering Chevron to pay US$ 18.2 billion in damages to the plaintiffs in that litigation.[216] As the tribunal noted, by far the "gravest allegation" raised in the arbitration was that the presiding judge, Nicolas Augusto Zambrano, corruptly agreed to

---

210 *Id.* ¶¶ 219–224.

211 *Id.* ¶¶ 225–226.

212 *Id.* ¶¶ 227, 349, 351 (finding that "the odds turned against the Claimant shortly after Deputy Prime Minister Sultanov left the Government").

213 *Id.* ¶¶ 325–327, 351–352.

214 White & Case LLP represented the Republic of Uzbekistan in this arbitration.

215 Vladislav Djanic, "In Newly Unearthed Uzbekistan Ruling, Exorbitant Fees Promised To Consultants On Eve Of Tender Process Are Viewed By Tribunal As Evidence Of Corruption, Leading To Dismissal Of All Claims Under Dutch BIT," IA Reporter, June 22, 2017 ("Djanic, Newly Unearthed Ruling").

216 *Chevron v. Ecuador* ¶¶ 4.442, 5.2.

allow the plaintiffs' representatives to "ghostwrite" the Lago Agrio judgment against Chevron and in the plaintiffs' favor.[217]

As to that allegation, the tribunal observed that, "[a]t least at first sight, particularly to a non-lawyer" unfamiliar with the long-running litigation, the Lago Agrio judgment "appears to be a lengthy, detailed, reasoned and powerful decision."[218] Nonetheless, the tribunal determined on a balance of probabilities that Judge Zambrano "actively solicited a bribe from whichever side" would be willing to pay him to issue a favorable judgment; that Chevron refused his approaches; that certain of the plaintiffs' representatives, especially Mr. Steven Donziger, a U.S. lawyer, and Mr. Pablo Fajardo Mendoza, an Ecuadorian lawyer, agreed to pay the requested bribes to Judge Zambrano from proceeds that would come from enforcing the judgment against Chevron; and that, in return for his promised reward, Judge Zambrano agreed to allow the plaintiffs' representatives to "ghostwrite" at least material parts of the judgment.[219]

In assessing the evidence, the tribunal noted that forensic images of two computers purportedly used by Judge Zambrano revealed "no 'smoking gun', but rather a mass of complex questions that cannot be answered on the limited forensic materials made available ... without much more evidence from other electronic devices available to Judge Zambrano, Mr Fajardo and others in Ecuador."[220] The tribunal likewise found "no direct factual evidence available in this arbitration proving definitively how and when" the judgment was drafted.[221] The tribunal thus relied on circumstantial evidence, which in its view was "overwhelming."[222]

As set out in the tribunal's partial award, a former Ecuadorian judge, Dr. Alberto Guerra Bastides, testified in U.S. court proceedings and as a witness for Chevron in the arbitration that Judge Zambrano had asked him to negotiate an agreement with Chevron's counsel to pay for a final judgment in Chevron's favor: "Mr Zambrano told me that Chevron would have much more money than the Plaintiffs for this agreement, and therefore we could get a better deal and greater profit for ourselves.... For several weeks I insisted on this

217 *Id.* ¶ 5.226.

218 *Id.* ¶¶ 5.3–5.4 (noting that the judgment was approximately 88,000 words extending 188 typed, single-spaced pages, divided into 15 parts with internal sub-sections).

219 *Id.* ¶¶ 5.230–5.232; *id.* ¶ 5.17.

220 *Id.* ¶ 6.106; *id.* ¶¶ 6.107, 6.110.

221 *Id.* ¶ 5.227 (finding that there was "much circumstantial evidence, both factual and non-forensic expert evidence," which, in the tribunal's view, "proves by whom it was *not* written and why and by whom it *was* written, at least in substantial and material part").

222 *Id.* ¶ 8.54.

deal with [a lawyer for Chevron], but he rejected my proposal and a relationship with Chevron was never achieved."[223]

Dr. Guerra further testified that, following Chevron's rejection of his bribe solicitation, Judge Zambrano reached an agreement with the plaintiffs' representatives "to quickly move the case along in their favor," and, to that end, Mr. Fajardo agreed to pay approximately US$ 1,000 per month to Dr. Guerra to ghostwrite court orders for Judge Zambrano to reject Chevron's procedural motions.[224] Dr. Guerra testified that the plaintiffs' representatives subsequently further agreed to pay US$ 500,000 to Judge Zambrano in return for allowing them to draft the Lago Agrio judgment, and that Judge Zambrano agreed to pay "a proper benefit" to Dr. Guerra for his assistance once that payment was made.[225] Dr. Guerra also testified that, approximately two weeks before the Lago Agrio judgment was issued, Judge Zambrano asked him to revise a draft judgment that he had received from Mr. Fajardo; that Dr. Guerra worked for two days revising that draft judgment in Judge Zambrano's residence using Mr. Fajardo's computer; that Judge Zambrano explicitly asked him not to make copies or leave traces of the document or the changes he was making; that the plaintiffs' lawyers thereafter made further changes to the draft judgment "up to the very last minute before it was published;" and that he subsequently assisted Judge Zambrano by phone in preparing a supplemental clarification order for the judgment.[226]

The tribunal found that Dr. Guerra's testimony was truthful and was "materially corroborated" by contemporaneous evidence.[227] Chevron, in fact, had commenced more than 20 actions in federal courts across the United States for alleged violations of a U.S. statute on racketeer influenced and corrupt organizations, which enabled Chevron to depose and cross-examine key witnesses, including Judge Zambrano and Mr. Donziger, and resulted in the disclosure of an "unprecedented mass of evidential material," including, among other things, Mr. Donziger's personal notebook, private email correspondence, computer hard drives, and hundreds of hours of video outtakes.[228] Prior to the disclosure of this evidence, the Lago Agrio plaintiffs' lawyers in Ecuador

---

223 *Id.* ¶¶ 4.347–4.349.

224 *Id.* ¶ 4.350.

225 *Id.* ¶¶ 4.405–4.408, 5.158.

226 *Id.* ¶¶ 5.157–5.158.

227 *Id.* ¶¶ 4.348–4.349, 4.351, 4.398–4.400 (describing, among other things, the contemporaneous affidavits of two lawyers for Chevron and of a person to whom they both reported).

228 *Id.* ¶¶ 4.326–4.327; *id.* ¶ 1.40 (noting that "the Parties had agreed that evidence adduced before the US Courts in the RICO Litigation, as filed in this arbitration with the Tribunal's approval, was to be treated as evidence in this arbitration").

noted with concern in an email to Mr. Donziger "that the effects are potentially devastating in Ecuador (apart from destroying the proceeding, all of us, your attorneys, might go to jail)," and that it was "NOT acceptable for the correspondence, the emails ... [to] be divulged."[229]

The emails obtained in the U.S. proceedings established that, at least two years before Judge Zambrano issued the Lago Agrio judgment, the plaintiffs' representatives repeatedly made veiled references to a covert plan to ghostwrite that judgment.[230] Forensic evidence, delivery records, and bank records also showed that various procedural orders were last saved on Dr. Guerra's computer before they were issued by Judge Zambrano with substantially identical text, that packages (likely containing the draft orders) were shipped from Dr. Guerra to a Lago Agrio court employee prior to Judge Zambrano's issuance of those orders, that US$ 1,000 was withdrawn on a monthly basis from a secret bank account maintained by the plaintiffs' representatives, and that corresponding sums of US$ 1,000 were then deposited into Dr. Guerra's bank account.[231]

In addition, while the forensic evidence was not itself dispositive in showing who drafted the Lago Agrio judgment, it showed that, as of the date on which the judgment was issued, no final draft or issued version of the judgment could be found on Judge Zambrano's computers.[232] Formatting differences in the text of the Lago Agrio judgment also were "consistent with blocks of text being cut or copied and pasted" from other documents.[233] Further, a linguistic expert assessed dozens of known writings by Judge Zambrano and determined that it was "highly probable" that the Lago Agrio judgment had multiple authors and that Judge Zambrano "did not author a significant amount" of the judgment.[234]

Moreover, a critical part of the damages calculation in the judgment could only be traced back to the report of a court-appointed "expert" and not to the

229 *Id.* ¶¶ 4.377–4.378 (finding that "[t]he reference to 'jail' was significant").

230 *Id.* ¶¶ 4.328, 4.332, 4.334, 4.337, 4.340–4.341.

231 *Id.* ¶¶ 4.352–4.375.

232 *Id.* ¶¶ 4.443, 6.36.

233 *Id.* ¶¶ 6.48, 6.110–6.111 (finding that there was "no way of knowing forensically where those blocks of text came from," and that "whilst the forensic evidence alone does not prove, on the balance of probabilities, that the Lago Agrio Judgment was corruptly 'ghostwritten' by one or more of the Lago Agrio Plaintiffs' representatives, it is more likely than not that the Judgment was drafted in material part on a computer or device other than the Zambrano Computers," which was consistent with and reinforced the tribunal's conclusion that "the Lago Agrio Judgment was at least in material part 'ghostwritten' by certain of the Lago Agrio Plaintiffs' representatives, in corrupt collusion with Judge Zambrano").

234 *Id.* ¶ 5.89; *id.* ¶ 5.90 (observing that the expert was not cross-examined and that the tribunal accorded weight to his testimony without finding it conclusive).

evidence on which the judgment falsely purported to rely.[235] It was undisputed that the alleged expert did not draft his report and that the plaintiffs' experts and consultants did.[236] In fact, Mr. Donziger's personal notebook and video outtakes of a meeting showed that the plaintiffs' representatives conspired to have the court appoint that expert, Mr. Richard Stalin Cabrera Vegan, with the intention of covertly ghostwriting his expert report and submitting it to the court on his behalf.[237] "Astonishingly," the tribunal observed, "all this was willingly recorded on film by the meeting's participants, including Mr Cabrera, Mr Fajardo and Mr Donziger."[238] Bank records also showed that the plaintiffs' representatives paid more than US$ 100,000 to Mr. Cabrera from their secret bank account.[239] The tribunal therefore concluded that the payments to Mr. Cabrera, as an auxiliary officer of the court, were bribes and were "part of the 'ghostwriting' exercise as a whole."[240]

Similarly, the Lago Agrio judgment relied on eight sets of other materials that were in the possession of the plaintiffs' representatives but were not filed with the Lago Agrio court or disclosed to or known by Chevron in the litigation, a troubling fact which Ecuador failed to explain.[241] The tribunal concluded that the Lago Agrio judgment thus made improper use of unfiled materials in the possession of the plaintiffs' representatives, and that "such use resulted from the corrupt conduct of Judge Zambrano in permitting certain of the Lago Agrio Plaintiffs' representatives to 'ghostwrite' material parts" of the judgment.[242]

Furthermore, while it tried to give Judge Zambrano "the benefit of any reasonable doubt," the tribunal reviewed the U.S. court transcripts of his testimony and determined that he "was a most unsatisfactory witness" who was not credible.[243] For example, Judge Zambrano testified that he had prepared the Lago Agrio judgment "all by himself" with the assistance of a student-secretary in less than three months, based on a court file of 237,000 pages that included more than 100 expert reports and many legal submissions, while also working

235 *Id.* ¶¶ 4.389, 5.119–5.120.

236 *Id.* ¶¶ 4.318, 4.473.

237 *Id.* ¶¶ 4.267–4.277 (quoting Mr. Fajardo's recorded statement that "our entire technical team ... of experts, scientists, attorneys, political scientists ... all will contribute to that [expert] report," which "isn't going to be the expert's," and Mr. Donziger's record statement that "[w]e could jack this thing up to thirty billion dollars in one day").

238 *Id.* ¶ 4.277.

239 *Id.* ¶¶ 4.300–4.301.

240 *Id.* ¶¶ 4.302–4.303, 5.245, 5.247.

241 *Id.* ¶¶ 5.33–5.34.

242 *Id.* ¶ 5.85.

243 *Id.* ¶¶ 5.149–5.150.

on other matters.[244] The tribunal found that, "whilst not absolutely impossible, this achievement within such a short time seems inherently unlikely" and raises "troubling questions" as to whether it was feasible for Judge Zambrano alone to review the voluminous court file and prepare the judgment in the time and manner he described.[245] Likewise, while Judge Zambrano testified that he dictated the judgment to his student-secretary without providing her written notes, the tribunal observed that the judgment contained "numbers, formulae and abbreviations that do not lend themselves to mere oral dictation," as well as "out of order numeric sequences identical to those in the unfiled materials which could not be the result of errors in dictation."[246]

The plaintiffs' representatives, especially Mr. Donziger and Mr. Fajardo, also had a clear motive. As the tribunal noted, the plaintiffs' lawyers, advisors, and funders would receive over US$ 5.7 billion of the judgment amount, including over US$ 1.1 billion for Mr. Donziger's firm, Donziger & Associates, and over US$ 363 million for Mr. Fajardo.[247]

Based on the totality of this evidence, the tribunal concluded that the plaintiffs' representatives had corruptly ghostwritten at least material parts of the Lago Agrio judgment by promising bribes to Judge Zambrano.[248] The tribunal further commented that, "[s]hort of a signed confession," the circumstantial evidence of the corrupt ghostwriting "must be the most thorough documentary, video, and testimonial proof of fraud ever put before an arbitral tribunal."[249]

Thus, while rare, corruption has been proven in several investment arbitrations. Below we consider the consequences for the claims where corruption is established.

---

244 *Id.* ¶¶ 5.10, 5.11.

245 *Id.* ¶¶ 5.11, 5.14–5.15. *See also id.* ¶ 4.54 (finding that Judge Zambrano was not experienced in handling and deciding civil cases, let alone large and complex cases).

246 *Id.* ¶ 5.138 (concluding that Judge Zambrano's account of his working methods was therefore "not credible").

247 *Id.* ¶¶ 4.411–4.412.

248 *Id.* ¶¶ 5.229–5.232 (further finding that the plaintiffs' representatives, especially Mr. Donziger and Mr. Fajardo, had "engaged in prolonged, malign conduct towards [Ecuador's] legal system generally and, particularly, the Lago Agrio Court in a manner that almost beggars belief in its arrogant contempt for elemental principles of truth and justice").

249 *Id.* ¶ 8.54. *See also id.* ¶ 4.482 (noting that Judge Kaplan of the U.S. District Court for the Southern District of New York similarly concluded that the Lago Agrio litigation was "sad" and "distressing" because "the course of justice was perverted" and the judgment "was obtained by corrupt means").

## VI The Consequences of Corruption in International Arbitration

As set out above, corruption is contrary to international public policy.[250] Thus, a State would violate its obligation to accord fair and equitable treatment by retaliating against and causing damage to an investor for failing to pay a bribe or for other corrupt reasons.

Conversely, if a party's claims arise under a contract or investment procured through corruption or concluded for purposes of paying a bribe, the claims arising out of that corrupt contract or investment would be dismissed. By contrast, if an investor made its investment lawfully and then later agreed to pay a bribe, the claims likely would be admitted and such post-investment bribery would be considered as part of the merits or quantum of the claims.

### 6.1 *Retaliating against and Causing Damage to an Investor for Corrupt Reasons Would Violate the State's Obligation to Accord Fair and Equitable Treatment*

A number of claimants in investment arbitrations have alleged that State officials solicited bribes and then retaliated against their investments for failing to comply with the bribe demand. While most of these claimants have failed to meet their burden of proof, as described in detail above, the tribunal in *Chevron v. Ecuador* determined that an Ecuadorian judge, Judge Zambrano, corruptly agreed to allow the plaintiffs' representatives to ghostwrite a court judgment in litigation brought against Chevron in Ecuador's Lago Agrio court.[251]

In considering whether such conduct amounted to a denial of justice and thus to a violation of Ecuador's obligation to accord fair and equitable treatment, the *Chevron* tribunal noted that the burden of proving a denial of justice is "not lightly discharged," as courts are presumed (subject to rebuttal) to have acted properly and are "permitted a margin of appreciation before the threshold of a denial of justice can be met."[252] Yet, as the tribunal explained, the corrupt ghostwriting of the Lago Agrio judgment evoked "the very gravest concerns as to judicial propriety," was "grossly improper by any moral, professional and legal standards," and "directly impacted, adversely," Chevron's

250 *See supra* § 2.

251 *See supra* § 5.

252 *Chevron v. Ecuador* ¶¶ 8.41–8.42; *id.* ¶ 8.40 ("There have been many shocks and surprises caused by court judgments in legal history, but without much more, amounting to discreditable improprieties and the failure of the whole national system, such judgments do not amount to a denial of justice.").

rights.[253] The tribunal accordingly determined that if the corrupt ghostwriting were attributable to Ecuador, it would amount to a denial of justice.[254]

As to the question of attribution, the tribunal observed that Judge Zambrano issued the Lago Agrio judgment in his capacity as a judge of the Lago Agrio court, which was part of Ecuador's judicial branch; that both he and Ecuador held him out as a judge acting in the name of Ecuador; that the Lago Agrio judgment was accorded the status of a judgment under Ecuadorian law; and that it was subject to enforcement and execution by Ecuador's judicial branch within Ecuador's national legal system.[255] The tribunal accordingly determined that Judge Zambrano's conduct in issuing the Lago Agrio judgment "was manifestly done 'cloaked with governmental authority.'"[256] The tribunal also found that Ecuador's appellate, cassation, and constitutional courts and its prosecutorial authorities had before them, in all material respects, "at least strong prima facie evidence of judicial misconduct, procedural fraud and (particularly) 'ghostwriting'" relating to the Lago Agrio judgment, but none of those courts or prosecutorial authorities took any appropriate steps to address the "justifiable concerns" or to comply with the tribunal's orders and interim awards to suspend enforcement of the judgment.[257] The tribunal determined that it therefore was not possible to treat Judge Zambrano's conduct "as private initiatives or personal frolics," and that there could be "no question" that his conduct was attributable to Ecuador.[258]

Quoting the decision of the ICJ in *ELSI v. Italy*, the *Chevron* tribunal accordingly found that the Lago Agrio judgment was "clearly improper and discreditable" and "was left unremedied" by Ecuador's courts and prosecutorial authorities, which "amounted to a failure of [Ecuador's] national system as a whole to satisfy minimum standards required under international law."[259] The tribunal therefore concluded that Ecuador had committed a denial of justice in violation of its obligation to accord both fair and equitable treatment and

253 *Id.* ¶ 8.59.

254 *Id.* ¶ 5.226 (noting that the corrupt ghostwriting of the judgment was "the origin of the injuries of which Claimants now complain under the Treaty").

255 *Id.* ¶¶ 8.46, 8.50.

256 *Id.* ¶ 8.50; *id.* ¶ 5.244 (finding that Judge Zambrano's corrupt ghostwriting was "the action of a judge within the scope of his professional duties" and "was plainly conduct attributable to the Respondent").

257 *Id.* ¶¶ 8.28, 8.34, 8.51.

258 *Id.* ¶¶ 8.51–8.52.

259 *Id.* ¶ 8.60.

the treatment required by customary international law under the applicable U.S.-Ecuador treaty.[260]

The tribunal further observed that "judicial bribery must rank as one of the more serious cases of corruption, striking directly at the rule of law, access to justice and public confidence in the legal system; and also, as regards the foreign enforcement of a corrupt judgment, at the law of nations."[261] The *Chevron* tribunal thus determined that, having been procured through judicial corruption, the Lago Agrio judgment (and the judgments of the appellate, cassation, and constitutional courts) violated international public policy and, therefore, as a matter of international comity "should not be recognised or enforced by the courts of other States."[262] Thus, while it reserved the issue of damages to a later stage of the arbitration, the tribunal ordered Ecuador, among other things, to take immediate steps to remove the status of enforceability from the Lago Agrio judgment; to preclude any of the Lago Agrio plaintiffs, any "trust" purporting to represent their interests, any of their representatives, or any non-party funder from enforcing any part of the judgment, directly or indirectly; to convey the tribunal's decision promptly in writing to any State where enforcement or recognition of the judgment may be sought; and to return promptly any proceeds that, notwithstanding the tribunal's orders, come into Ecuador's custody, possession, or control.[263]

For the same public policy reasons, the U.S. District Court for the Southern District of New York similarly held that, having obtained the Lago Agrio judgment through corruption, the Lago Agrio plaintiffs' representatives "may not be allowed to benefit from that in any way."[264] Thus, in order to "prevent them from doing so," the court, among other things, imposed a constructive trust for Chevron's benefit on all property that either Mr. Donziger or the Lago Agrio plaintiffs' representatives had received or may receive, directly or indirectly, as a result of any right, title, or interest traceable to the judgment or its enforcement "anywhere in the world," and further ordered that Mr. Donziger and the

260 *Id.* ¶¶ 8.77, 10.5. *See also id.* ¶ 8.24 ("There is a consistent line of awards over many years, amounting to a *jurisprudence constant*, deciding that a denial of justice in violation of customary international law will also amount to a breach of an FET standard in a treaty.").

261 *Id.* ¶ 9.16.

262 *Id. See also id.* ¶ 9.17 (holding that "the reinstatement of the Claimants' rights under international law requires of [Ecuador] the immediate suspension of the enforceability of the Lago Agrio Judgment and the implementation of such other corrective measures as are necessary to 'wipe out all the consequences' of [Ecuador's] internationally wrongful acts, so as to re-establish the situation which would have existed if those internationally wrongful acts had not been committed by [Ecuador]").

263 *Id.* ¶ 10.13.

264 *Id.* ¶ 4.482.

Lago Agrio plaintiffs "shall transfer and forthwith assign to Chevron all such property" that he or they had obtained or thereafter may obtain.[265]

Other investors have raised similar claims, but have failed to prove the alleged bribe or a causal connection between the bribe and any State action that caused them damage. For example, the claimants in two ICSID cases, *Liman v. Kazakhstan* and *Rumeli v. Kazakhstan*, both argued generally that the courts of Kazakhstan were corrupt and that the court decisions in those cases were so arbitrary that they must have been the result of corruption, bias, and bad faith. Consistent with the *Chevron* decision, the *Liman* tribunal observed that "corruption is a serious allegation, especially in the context of the judiciary," and that, if found, such corruption "would constitute a grave violation" of the obligation to accord fair and equitable treatment.[266] The tribunals in both *Liman* and *Rumeli* concluded, however, that the generalized allegations made against Kazakhstan's judiciary were insufficient to prove corruption and that other more particularized allegations were unsupported by the record.[267]

In the ICSID case of *F-W Oil v. Trinidad & Tobago*, F-W Oil argued in its written submissions that officials of State enterprises corruptly retaliated against F-W Oil for refusing to pay a US$ 1.5 million bribe allegedly demanded in connection with an oil and gas contract.[268] The tribunal noted that it was "naturally much concerned from the outset" about these allegations, and that any ICSID tribunal "is bound to take the most serious view of allegations of State corruption—if backed by proper evidence."[269] As the tribunal explained, corruption has a "dire and pernicious effect" on economic development, particularly in developing countries, "and economic development is after all the purpose which Bilateral Investment Treaties and the World Bank itself were created to serve."[270] The tribunal therefore confirmed that, "if allegations of corruption had been made and had proved to be well founded, it would have had a most substantial effect on the view of the case taken by the Tribunal, and most particularly so if and when it came to the point at which the actions or omissions of the State came to be measured against the standard of treatment for foreign investment laid down in the BIT."[271]

265 *Id.* ¶¶ 4.482–4.483.

266 *Liman v. Kazakhstan* ¶ 422.

267 *Id.* ¶¶ 422–424; *Rumeli v. Kazakhstan* ¶¶ 653–655.

268 *F-W Oil Interests, Inc. v. Republic of Trinidad & Tobago*, ICSID Case No. ARB/01/14, Award dated Mar. 3, 2006 ¶¶ 14, 36, 41.

269 *Id.* ¶¶ 211–212.

270 *Id.* ¶ 212.

271 *Id.*

As the *F-W Oil* tribunal further explained, however, F-W Oil withdrew its bribery allegations at the end of the hearing and asked the tribunal not to rule on them.[272] The tribunal accordingly concluded that, in view of F-W Oil's abandonment of its bribery allegations, it had no reason to rule on them and "every reason why it should not."[273]

In the ICSID case of *EDF v. Romania*, EDF claimed that its contract to operate duty free shops at Romania's airports was not extended beyond its ten-year term because EDF had refused to pay a US$ 2.5 million bribe allegedly demanded by two officials in the office of the Prime Minister of Romania.[274] The tribunal agreed with EDF that "a request for a bribe by a State agency is a violation of the fair and equitable treatment obligation" and "a violation of international public policy, and that exercising a State's discretion on the basis of corruption is a … fundamental breach of transparency and legitimate expectations."[275] The tribunal rejected EDF's claims, however, finding that EDF had failed to meet its burden of proving the bribery allegations as the evidence proffered was "far from being clear and convincing."[276]

In *ECE Projektmanagement v. Czech Republic*, the claimants alleged that State officials had obstructed administrative permitting procedures for their shopping center project and had granted preferential treatment to their competitor's project because that competitor had paid bribes.[277] The *ECE Projektmanagement* tribunal observed that "[i]nternational tribunals cannot turn a blind eye to corruption and cannot decline to investigate the matter simply because of the difficulties of proof."[278] Following a detailed review of the allegations, however, the tribunal did not find any substantial evidence

272 *Id.* ¶ 49, fn. 4; *id.* ¶¶ 138, 210 (observing that "the allegations of fraud and corruption progressively withered away, leaving only vestiges behind," and were "ultimately withdrawn at the very end of the hearing, under pointed questioning from the Tribunal itself as to whether there was any real evidence to sustain allegations of that breadth and gravity").

273 *Id.* ¶ 211 (further noting that it had prepared "an elaborate account of the documents and evidence devoted to every aspect of this unhappy story," but that, in the end, it "decided that no useful purpose would be served by including it, and that to do so risked being positively harmful, since in the absence of an express finding by the Tribunal definitively rejecting the charges a reader might be tempted to assume, especially in relation to the two or three named persons who were specially subjected to attack, that there was (as the saying goes) 'no smoke without fire'").

274 *EDF v. Romania* ¶¶ 71–72, 221.

275 *Id.* ¶ 221.

276 *Id. See also id.* ¶¶ 222–237.

277 *ECE Projektmanagement v. Czech Republic* ¶¶ 4.392–4.393, 4.719.

278 *Id.* ¶ 4.871.

of any individual acts of corruption or of an alleged corruption "scheme" and therefore rejected the allegations.[279]

In the ICSID case of *H&H v. Egypt*, H&H argued that officials in two State-owned companies had solicited bribes and that Egypt's State apparatus had failed to take any measures against the officials who solicited those bribes.[280] The tribunal found that there was "no evidence" that any alleged bribe solicitations by the State-owned companies were attributable to Egypt.[281] Moreover, the tribunal concluded that, even if it accepted the corruption allegations at face value and even further assuming that Egypt had failed to take necessary measures against the officials who allegedly solicited bribes, H&H also would need to establish that the bribe solicitations caused damage to its investment, which in the tribunal's assessment H&H had failed to do.[282] The tribunal therefore rejected the claims finding that H&H had failed to establish a causal link between the alleged bribery solicitation and the alleged loss of its investment.[283]

Finally, in the ICSID case of *RSM v. Grenada*, RSM brought arbitration claims contesting the rejection of its application for an oil and gas exploration license. In parallel with the arbitration, RSM filed a complaint in U.S. court accusing a particular government official and other individuals of corruption allegedly causing over US$ 500 million in damages.[284] By contrast, in the arbitration, RSM accused that same official of dishonesty and incompetence, but did not claim that he had engaged in corruption.[285] The *RSM* tribunal accordingly did not make any finding of corruption and, on the merits, it found that RSM had lost its right to obtain the exploration license at issue due to its own failure to submit a timely application for the license.[286]

Following the rejection of its claims, RSM and its shareholders brought a second arbitration claiming that they had obtained new evidence that RSM was "forced out" because a competitor had paid a bribe to the same official

279 *Id.* ¶¶ 4.931, 4.932 (observing that the claimants' evidence was "far from reaching a sufficient level of cogency," and that the disputed State measures "in all instances were comprehensible and not unreasonable in the circumstances in which each decision was made").

280 *H&H v. Egypt* ¶ 389.

281 *Id.* ¶ 391.

282 *Id.* ¶¶ 392–393.

283 *Id.* ¶¶ 395–399 (finding that the evidence showed that H&H "was unable to realize its investment for reasons of its own inability to fulfill its obligations").

284 *RSM Production Corp. v. Grenada*, ICSID Case No. ARB/05/14, Award dated Mar. 13, 2009 ¶ 30.

285 *Id.* ¶ 212.

286 *Id.* ¶¶ 212, 502.

accused in the earlier U.S. court proceedings.[287] The second tribunal concluded that RSM's claims were manifestly without legal merit and were "no more than an attempt to re-litigate and overturn the findings of another ICSID tribunal, based on allegations of corruption that were either known at the time or which ought to have been raised by way of a revision application and over which the Prior Tribunal had jurisdiction."[288]

As the *RSM* tribunal explained, moreover, the corruption allegations, if proven, "would certainly show that certain Grenadian government officials had acted unlawfully under Grenadian and international law (the acceptance of a bribe being unlawful under both)," but such illegality, by itself, would not amount to a treaty violation.[289] Indeed, as the tribunal emphasized, the first arbitration had established definitively that RSM's license application was untimely and that Grenada therefore had acted properly in rejecting it.[290] The tribunal therefore concluded that, even if the corruption allegations were accepted, the claims would fail due to a lack of causation, as RSM needed to show that Grenada took action "as it was improperly bidden" to do and thereby caused damage to RSM, which was not alleged let alone proven.[291]

In sum, in accordance with well-settled public policy, a State would violate its obligation to accord fair and equitable treatment if it retaliated against and caused damage to an investor for failing to pay a bribe or for other corrupt reasons. To prevail in establishing such a violation, however, the investor must not only prove the alleged corruption—which is inherently difficult to do—but also must show that such corruption was attributable to the State and resulted in action taken by the State that caused it damage.

### 6.2 *Claims Arising out of Contracts Procured through Corruption or Concluded for Purposes of Paying Bribes Would Be Dismissed*

It is more common in international arbitration for the respondent to raise corruption as a defense to the claims.[292] In both commercial and investment

287 *Rachel S. Grynberg, Stephen M. Grynberg, Miriam Z. Grynberg, and RSM Production Corp. v. Grenada*, ICSID Case No. ARB/10/6, Award dated Dec. 10, 2010 ¶¶ 5.1.3–5.1.4.

288 *Id.* ¶¶ 7.1.18, 7.3.3–7.3.6.

289 *Id.* ¶ 7.2.6.

290 *Id.* ¶¶ 7.2.5, 7.2.21.

291 *Id.* ¶¶ 7.2.5, 7.27, 7.2.21.

292 *See, e.g.*, Claus von Wobeser, "The Corruption Defense and Preserving the Rule of Law," *in* INTERNATIONAL ARBITRATION AND THE RULE OF LAW: CONTRIBUTION AND CONFORMITY COMMENTARY 2017 at 204 ("Respondent host states (in great majority) have taken notice and advanced corruption arguments to attempt voiding a contract, or argue that the tribunal lacks jurisdiction, or allege that the claims are inadmissible."); Aloysius Llamzon and Anthony Sinclair, "Investor Wrongdoing in Investment Arbitration:

arbitrations, tribunals consistently have held that contracts to pay bribes are void and that contracts procured through corruption are, at a minimum, voidable. Such contracts therefore would not give rise to valid claims.

The seminal case, ICC Case No. 1110 of 1963, took place over a half century ago in France before a sole arbitrator, the late Judge Gunnar Lagergren, who later served as the first president of the Iran-U.S. Claims Tribunal and as a judge on the European Court of Human Rights. In that case, both parties affirmed that their contractual undertakings in Argentina were valid and binding under French law and that Judge Lagergren had jurisdiction.[293] Judge Lagergren determined, however, that the commissions under the contract were primarily to bribe Argentine officials, and that "[s]uch corruption is an international evil; it is contrary to good morals and to an international public policy common to the community of nations."[294] Judge Lagergren therefore decided on his own motion that he lacked jurisdiction:

> After weighing all the evidence I am convinced that a case such as this, involving such gross violation of good morals and international public policy, can have no countenance in any court either in the Argentine or in France, or, for that matter, in any other civilised country, nor in any arbitral tribunal. Thus, jurisdiction must be declined in this case.... Parties who ally themselves in an enterprise of the present nature must realise that they have forfeited any right to ask for assistance of the machinery of justice (national courts or arbitral tribunals) in settling their disputes.[295]

More recently, the tribunal in ICC Case No. 13384 similarly commented:

> [T]here is no doubt that corruption is worldwide considered a wrongful and, indeed, unacceptable practice which is condemned by various international conventions, instruments of international organizations such as UN, UNCITRAL, OECD, European Union etc. not to mention national

---

Standards Governing Issues of Corruption, Fraud, Misrepresentation and Other Investor Misconduct," *in* Albert J. van den Berg, LEGITIMACY: MYTHS, REALITIES, CHALLENGES, 2015 at 451 (observing that such bribery and fraud defenses are "now common").

293 ICC Case No. 1110, Award of 1963, YCA 1996 ¶¶ 2–4.

294 *Id.* ¶¶ 17–18, 20. *See also id.* ¶ 7 (observing "that while infringements of foreign customs or exchange laws, tax statutes and other similar provisions may be immaterial from the point of view of French public policy, there can hardly be any doubt that French public policy will not ignore more serious violations of foreign laws involving grave offences to good morals").

295 *Id.* ¶¶ 2, 23.

> legislations.... Condemnation of such practice may in effect be seen as a material rule of international public policy, indeed a rule of 'transnational or truly international public policy' (to use an expression today common in the international legal community) which must apply irrespective of whichever national law parties to a contract may have chosen to govern it.[296]

Consistent with these observations, tribunals in a number of ICC cases have rejected claims arising out of contracts obtained by corruption or concluded for the purpose of paying bribes, irrespective of the national law that applied in those cases. For example:

- In ICC Case No. 3916, the sole arbitrator found that the contract between the parties was concluded for the purpose of paying bribes and exercising undue influence to obtain approvals from the government of Iran and therefore was null and void under the applicable French law. As the sole arbitrator explained, while the bribes were paid to foreign officials in another country, French law "is not limited to considering as illegal and/or against public order corruption of French public officials or the undue influence exercised upon them, but corruption and undue influence in general."[297]
- In ICC Case No. 6497, the tribunal determined that the real purpose of one particular agreement between the parties was to channel bribes and that it therefore was null and void under the applicable Swiss law. The tribunal explained that "bribes in themselves cannot be, in Swiss law, the object of a valid contract," a principle which "is also admitted in most legal systems," and it therefore rejected the claims arising under that agreement.[298]
- In ICC Case No. 8891, the tribunal found that the true intention of the parties in concluding their contract was to pay bribes. Under the applicable French law, the tribunal therefore dismissed the claims and observed that "the payment of 'bribes' ... is, in French law, illegal and immoral.... This solution is not only in conformity with the internal French public order, it also results from the conception of international public policy as most nations recognize it."[299]

---

296 ICC Case No. 13384, Award dated Dec. 2005, *ICC Bulletin (Supplement)* 24 (2013) 62 ¶ 65.

297 ICC Award No. 3916 of 1982, Collection of ICC Arbitral Awards 1974–1985 at 510 (unofficial translation) ("[*Le droit Français*] *ne se limite pas de considérer comme illicite et/ou contrevenant aux bonnes mœurs la corruption des fonctionnaires français ou le trafic d'influence sur ceux-ci, mais la corruption des fonctionnaires français ou le trafic d'influence tout court.*").

298 ICC Case No. 6497 ¶¶ 2, 30.

299 ICC Case No. 8891 at 562 (unofficial translation) ("*le versement de « pots-de-vin » ... est, en droit français, illicite et immorale ... Cette solution n'est pas seulement conforme à l'ordre*

- In ICC Case No. 12990, the tribunal determined that the claimant had paid bribes on behalf of the respondent to obtain a petrol purchase contract. Applying French law, the tribunal therefore dismissed the claimant's claims to be paid for its services and remarked that, "whether it be under French law or international public policy rules, corruption is illicit," and "a contract that has an illicit consideration or has been induced by an illicit consideration is null and void."[300]
- In ICC Case No. 13515, the tribunal determined that the respondent had paid the claimant to make illegal payments to obtain the award of a government contract. The tribunal held that the contract therefore was void due to corruption under both French law and international public policy, and, consequently, it dismissed both parties' claims, concluding that the claimant could not be awarded any unpaid commissions and the respondent could not be refunded the amounts it had paid under the contract.[301]
- In ICC Case No. 13914, the tribunal found that the payments made by the respondent to the claimant under their consulting agreement were bribes. The tribunal observed that "arbitration precedents and legal authorities dealing with bribery and corruption are clear: If bribery is established by the evidence to have been part of the intent of, and in fact arises out of, a consulting agreement, such agreement is to be declared null and void *ab initio*."[302] The tribunal therefore declared the parties' consulting agreement null and void under the applicable Texas state law and U.S. federal law and dismissed the claims.[303]

The ICSID tribunal in *World Duty Free v. Kenya*, an investment arbitration brought pursuant to a contract, dismissed the claims in that case for the same public policy reasons. As discussed above, World Duty Free's CEO admitted paying a "personal donation" to the President of Kenya to obtain the contract underlying the claims, and the tribunal concluded that such payment was a

*public français interne, elle résulte également de la conception de l'ordre public international tel que la plupart des nations le reconnait.*").

300 ICC Case No. 12990 ¶¶ 193, 343 (English translation).

301 ICC Case No. 13515 at 67 ("*Le tribunal arbitral a considéré qu'un contrat entaché de corruption n'était pas valide; tant au regard du droit français ... que de l'ordre public international; et a examiné en l'espèce les circonstances prouvant la corruption.... Il a conclu que le contrat était nul car entaché de corruption et qu'en conséquence la demanderesse ne pouvait prétendre au versement des commissions impayées; ni la défenderesse au remboursement des sommes déboursées.*").

302 ICC Case No. 13914, Final Award dated Mar. 2008, 24 *ICC Bulletin* (*Supplement*) 77 (2013) ¶ 238 (observing that "[n]either party may require performance of the contract nor seek restitution under it").

303 *Id.* ¶¶ 239–240.

bribe.[304] As also discussed above, the *World Duty Free* tribunal concluded that "bribery is contrary to the international public policy of most, if not all, States or, to use another formula, to transnational public policy," and, consequently, that "claims based on contracts of corruption or on contracts obtained by corruption cannot be upheld by this Arbitral Tribunal."[305]

The contract in *World Duty Free* provided that it was governed by Kenyan law and that any tribunal constituted under the contract was bound to apply English law.[306] While noting that these provisions were "perhaps awkwardly worded," the tribunal found "no practical difficulty" because there was "no material difference on the specific points at issue between the position at common law in England and Kenya."[307] The tribunal explained:

> In the Tribunal's view, it is significant that in England, historically, the common law has traditionally abhorred the corruption by bribery of officers of state, ranking its offence next to high treason. Such corruption is more odious than theft; but it does not depend upon any financial loss and it requires no immediate victim. Corruption of a state officer by bribery is synonymous with the most heinous crimes because it can cause huge economic damage; and its long-term victims can be legion. The offence lies in bribing a person to exercise his public duty corruptly and not in accordance with what is right and proper for the state and its citizens. Like any other contract, a state contract procured by bribing a state officer is legally unenforceable, as an affront to the public conscience. The fact that the transaction is performed outside England or is subject to a law other than English law is immaterial.... In the Tribunal's view, this same statement describes the converse position at common law in Kenya.[308]

The *World Duty Free* tribunal concluded that the contract was voidable under both English law and Kenyan law, and that Kenya in fact did avoid the agreement through its written submissions after learning of the bribe during the arbitration.[309] The tribunal further concluded that World Duty Free also was "not legally entitled to maintain any of its pleaded claims in these proceedings as a matter of *ordre public international* and public policy under the contract's

304 *See supra* § 5.

305 *See supra* § 6.2; *World Duty Free v. Kenya* ¶ 157.

306 *Id.* ¶ 158.

307 *Id.* ¶ 159.

308 *Id.* ¶ 173.

309 *Id.* ¶ 188(1).

applicable laws."[310] The tribunal therefore dismissed the claims and ordered both parties to bear their own costs of the arbitration, including legal costs.[311]

Notably, after it lost the arbitration, World Duty Free submitted new arbitration claims against Kenya's airports authority under the same contract. In that second ad hoc arbitration, the airports authority did not raise corruption as a defense, and the sole arbitrator found the airports authority liable and awarded damages of over US$ 44 million to World Duty Free. The airports authority contested the award and argued that the High Court of Kenya should set it aside because, among other things, the prior tribunal already had determined that the contract was procured by corruption and therefore was void.[312] The High Court noted that Kenya's arbitration act "frowns upon an Award that is contrary to Public Policy" and thus is "a prescription to Arbitral Tribunals that however much their Awards should enjoy autonomy, they will not be tolerated as long as they are inimical to Public Policy."[313] The High Court further observed:

> [I]t is for this reason that once it is brought to the attention of an Arbitral Tribunal (even if not pleaded) that it is about to make a pronouncement that runs against Public Policy, then the Tribunal ought to pause and interrogate the allegation so as not to cross the Red line.
>
> Had the [sole arbitrator] done so then it would have been obvious that to allow the claim in the manner that [he] did was to approve a claim whose very foundation had been declared to have been obtained through Bribery and Corruption by a Tribunal whose Decisions are taken to have the binding force of a final Judgment of Court in Kenya.[314]

The High Court accordingly held that "the Award cannot stand and must be set aside," and it chastised World Duty Free for "some act of boldness" in submitting claims under the same contract that already had been declared illegal by the first *World Duty Free* tribunal.[315]

Finally, in the ICSID case of *Niko v. Bangladesh*, Niko brought claims against Bangladesh and two State agencies or instrumentalities, BAPEX and Petrobangla, under a joint venture agreement concluded by Niko and BAPEX

310 *Id.* ¶ 188(3).

311 *Id.* ¶ 192.

312 *Kenya Airports Authority v. World Duty Free Co. Ltd.*, High Court of Kenya Misc. Application No. 67 of 2013, Ruling dated Oct. 5, 2018 ¶ 16.

313 *Id.* ¶ 38.

314 *Id.* ¶¶ 38–39.

315 *Id.* ¶¶ 39–40.

and under a gas purchase and sale agreement subsequently concluded by Niko, BAPEX, and Petrobangla with the approval of the Government of Bangladesh. As the tribunal explained, it was uncontested that, following the conclusion of the joint venture agreement and prior to the conclusion of the gas purchase and sale agreement, Niko provided undue benefits to bribe Bangladesh's then State Minister for Energy and Mineral Resources, Mr. Mosharaf Hossain.[316] Indeed, Niko's parent company pleaded guilty in Canada and admitted in an "Agreed Statement of Facts" that Niko had purchased a Toyota Land Cruiser for CAD 190,984 and had paid travel expenses for Minister Hossain in order to persuade him to use his influence to ensure that Niko secured the gas purchase and sale agreement.[317]

In assessing the effect of this admitted act of bribery on the claims, the *Niko* tribunal confirmed that a contract having influence peddling or bribery as its objective is "in conflict with international public policy" and, consequently, is void or unenforceable and "cannot be given effect by arbitrators."[318] As the tribunal explained, however, the claims in that case arose out of two agreements relating to the development of gas fields and the sale of gas from such fields, and there was nothing illegal about the object or content of those agreements.[319]

As to the further question of whether either agreement was obtained through corruption, the *Niko* tribunal observed that the joint venture agreement was concluded long before the corrupt acts took place.[320] The tribunal also found that Niko's corruption of Minister Hossain "soon became known in Bangladesh and was publicised in the press," that Minister Hossain promptly resigned, and that the gas purchase and sale agreement was concluded "some 18 months later."[321] The tribunal thus concluded that there was "no link of causation between the established acts of corruption and the conclusion of the agreements, and it is not alleged that there is such a link."[322]

The *Niko* tribunal further observed that "the consequences of corruption may lead to the annulment or rescission of a contract, the withdrawal of such rights as a concession; but these consequences are not automatic."[323] As the tribunal explained, an innocent victim of illegality must have the choice either

316 *Niko v. Bangladesh* ¶ 382.
317 *Id.* ¶¶ 383–389.
318 *Id.* ¶¶ 434, 436.
319 *Id.* ¶ 438.
320 *Id.* ¶ 454.
321 *Id.* ¶¶ 387, 454.
322 *Id.* ¶ 455.
323 *Id.* ¶ 447.

to accept the transaction in the terms concluded or to avoid it.[324] The *Niko* tribunal emphasized that, in contrast to Kenya's unequivocal avoidance of its contract in *World Duty Free*, Bangladesh, BAPEX, and Petrobangla did not avoid either agreement underlying the claims, but instead continued to enjoy the benefits of those agreements.[325] The *Niko* tribunal therefore concluded that, in the absence of a clear declaration by the respondents avoiding the agreements or of any illegality in the content or performance of either agreement, the tribunal "may not now treat the Agreements as avoided or invalid."[326]

The authorities set out above thus show that a contract concluded for purposes of paying bribes is null and void, and a contract obtained through corruption is voidable.

### 6.3 *Investments Made through Corruption Would Not Be Protected under Any Treaty and Would Not Give Rise to Valid Claims*

In investment treaty arbitrations, investments made through corruption would not be protected and would not give rise to valid claims.

Many investment treaties, in fact, contain clauses providing that the investor must make its investment in compliance with law in order to benefit from the treaty's protections.[327] Where claims have arisen under an investment treaty containing such a clause and it was proven that the investment was made unlawfully, tribunals have refused jurisdiction. For example, the ICSID tribunal in *Inceysa v. El Salvador* observed that a clause in the Spain-El Salvador BIT underlying the claims in that case required the investor to make its investment "in accordance with law," which demonstrated "the clear and obvious intent of the signatory States to exclude from its protection investments made in violation of the internal laws of each of them."[328] The *Inceysa* tribunal further remarked:

> [T]he inclusion of the clause 'in accordance with law' in the agreements for reciprocal protection of investments follows international public policies designed to sanction illegal acts and their resulting effects.

324 *Id.* ¶ 451 (finding that "the victim should not be sanctioned for the other party's illegality by being deprived of the bargain struck which it might find to its advantage").

325 *Id.* ¶¶ 456–463.

326 *Id.* ¶ 464. *See also id.* ¶¶ 484–485.

327 Carolyn B. Lamm, Brody K. Greenwald, and Kristen M. Young, "From *World Duty Free* to *Metal-Tech*: A Review of International Investment Treaty Arbitration Cases Involving Allegations of Corruption," ICSID REVIEW, Vol. 29, No. 2 (2014) at 342–345.

328 *Inceysa Vallisoletana, S.L. v. Republic of El Salvador*, ICSID Case No. ARB/03/26, Award dated Aug. 2, 2006 ¶ 246.

> It is uncontroversial that respect for the law is a matter of public policy not only in El Salvador, but in any civilized country....
>
> The Tribunal agrees with El Salvador and notes that an interpretation of the Agreement that would afford protection to investments made fraudulently would have enormous repercussions for those States which signed agreements for reciprocal protection of investments and included the clause 'in accordance with law,' in order to exclude from the protection of said treaties the investments not made in accordance with the laws and other norms of the State that receives the investment.[329]

On the facts of the case, the *Inceysa* tribunal found that Inceysa had made misrepresentations during the public bidding process to obtain its concession contract, including with respect to the identity of its strategic partner, which was "a deceit on one of the central aspects of the bid."[330] The tribunal accordingly concluded that "Inceysa's investment was made in a manner that was clearly illegal" and, consequently, that El Salvador had not consented to arbitrate the dispute and the tribunal therefore lacked jurisdiction to resolve it.[331]

The tribunal in *Anderson v. Costa Rica*, an ICSID additional facility arbitration, likewise held that the inclusion of a similar clause in the Canada-Costa Rica BIT underlying the claims in that case was a "clear indication of the importance that [the State parties] attached to the legality of the investments made by investors of the other Party and their intention that their laws with respect to investments be strictly followed."[332] The *Anderson* tribunal explained:

> The Tribunal's interpretation of the words 'owned in accordance with the laws' of Costa Rica reflects both sound public policy and sound investment practice. Costa Rica, indeed any country, has a fundamental interest in securing respect for its law. It clearly sought to secure that interest by requiring investments under the BIT to be owned and controlled according to law. At the same time, prudent investment practice requires that

329 *Id.* ¶¶ 247–248, 250.

330 *Id.* ¶ 123; *id.* ¶¶ 239, 242–243, 252–253 (finding that Inceysa thus violated, among other things, the principle of good faith, the principle that no one should be permitted to profit from their own fraud, international public policy, and the prohibition against unlawful enrichment, all of which were incorporated into Salvadoran law).

331 *Id.* ¶ 257 (the tribunal declaring itself "incompetent to hear the dispute brought before it").

332 *Alasdair Ross Anderson, et al. v. Republic of Costa Rica*, ICSID Case No. ARB(AF)/07/3, Award dated May 19, 2010 ¶ 53 (further noting that "[t]he assurance of legality with respect to investment has important, indeed crucial, consequences for the public welfare and economic well-being of any country").

> any investor exercise due diligence before committing funds to any particular investment proposal. An important element of such due diligence is for investors to assure themselves that their investments comply with the law. Such due diligence obligation is neither overly onerous nor unreasonable.[333]

The *Anderson* tribunal found that the entire transaction constituting the claimants' investment was an illegal Ponzi scheme such that the claimants "did not own their investments in accordance with the laws of Costa Rica."[334] The tribunal therefore concluded that it lacked jurisdiction.[335]

Similarly, in the first *Fraport v. Philippines* arbitration, the ICSID tribunal determined that the Germany-Philippines BIT underlying the claims "explicitly and reiteratedly required that an investment, in order to qualify for BIT protection, had to be in accordance with the host state's law," and that Fraport "knowingly and intentionally" had made its investment in violation of a Philippine anti-dummy law "by means of secret shareholder agreements."[336] The tribunal concluded that Fraport thus had failed to comply with the "explicit and hardly unreasonable" legality requirement contained in the BIT, which deprived the tribunal of jurisdiction.[337] Although an ad hoc committee subsequently annulled the tribunal's award, the ICSID tribunal in the resubmitted proceeding also found that Fraport had violated the anti-dummy law when making its investment, which therefore was not "protected by the BIT because of its illegality."[338] Thus, as in the first case, the tribunal in the second case held that the Philippines had not consented to arbitrate the dispute and that it therefore lacked jurisdiction.[339]

The ICSID tribunal in *Metal-Tech v. Uzbekistan* refused jurisdiction under the Israel-Uzbekistan BIT in the first investment treaty arbitration ever dismissed on grounds of corruption. As the *Metal-Tech* tribunal noted, Israel and Uzbekistan had limited the scope of their consent in the BIT to arbitrate only disputes arising out of investments implemented in accordance with local law.[340] This "legality requirement," as the tribunal explained, excluded from the

---

333 *Id.* ¶ 58.

334 *Id.*

335 *Id.* ¶ 59.

336 *Fraport AG Frankfurt Airport Services Worldwide v. Republic of the Philippines*, ICSID Case No. ARB/03/25, Award dated Aug. 16, 2007 ("*Fraport v. Philippines I*") ¶¶ 398, 401.

337 *Id.* ¶ 404.

338 *Id.* ¶ 467.

339 *Id.*

340 *Metal-Tech v. Uzbekistan* ¶ 164.

BIT's protection investments made through non-trivial violations of the host State's laws, violations of its foreign investment regime, fraud, and corruption.[341]

As discussed in detail above, the *Metal-Tech* tribunal found that Metal-Tech had paid bribes to the brother of the Prime Minister of Uzbekistan and to a government official to make its investment.[342] Having thus determined that Metal-Tech had made its investment in violation of Uzbek law contrary to the BIT's requirements, the *Metal-Tech* tribunal concluded that Uzbekistan had not consented to arbitrate under either the BIT or the ICSID Convention, and that, in the absence of such consent, the tribunal lacked jurisdiction over the dispute.[343]

Many treaties, however, do not expressly condition their protections on the investor making its investment in accordance with law. In such cases, tribunals have expressed differing views as to whether the legality of the investment is an implicit requirement. In *Plama v. Bulgaria*, for example, Plama brought its claims under the Energy Charter Treaty ("ECT"), which does not include an express legality requirement. The *Plama* tribunal nonetheless held that the ECT's protections applied only to investments made in compliance with law:

> Unlike a number of Bilateral Investment Treaties, the ECT does not contain a provision requiring the conformity of the Investment with a particular law. This does not mean, however, that the protections provided for by the ECT cover all kinds of investments, including those contrary to domestic or international law….
>
> In accordance with the introductory note to the ECT '[t]he fundamental aim of the Energy Charter Treaty is to strengthen the rule of law on energy issues […]'. Consequently, the ECT should be interpreted in a manner consistent with the aim of encouraging respect for the rule of law. The Arbitral Tribunal concludes that the substantive protections of the ECT cannot apply to investments that are made contrary to law.[344]

The *Plama* tribunal found that Plama had made its investment by misrepresenting the identity of the investors during the privatization process, which was "a deliberate concealment amounting to fraud, calculated to induce the Bulgarian authorities to authorize the transfer of shares to an entity that did

341 *Id.* ¶ 165.

342 *See supra* § 5.

343 *Metal-Tech v. Uzbekistan* ¶ 373.

344 *Plama Consortium Ltd. v. Republic of Bulgaria*, ICSID Case No. ARB/03/24, Award dated Aug. 27, 2008 ¶¶ 138–139. White & Case represented the Republic of Bulgaria in this arbitration.

not have the financial and managerial capacities required to resume operation of the Refinery."[345] As the tribunal explained, granting the ECT's protections to such an investment would be contrary to Bulgarian law, to the principle of *nemo auditur propriam turpitudinem allegans* (no one can be heard to invoke his own turpitude), to "the basic notion of international public policy—that a contract obtained by wrongful means (fraudulent misrepresentation) should not be enforced by a tribunal," and to "the principle of good faith which is part not only of Bulgarian law ... but also of international law…."[346] The tribunal accordingly concluded that Plama was not entitled to the ECT's protections and dismissed all of the claims.[347]

In the past decade, a growing number of tribunals similarly have held that investment treaties generally and the ICSID Convention in particular implicitly condition their protection on the investor making its investment in compliance with law. For example:

- The ICSID tribunal in *Phoenix Action v. Czech Republic* explained that "[t]he purpose of the international mechanism of protection of investment through ICSID arbitration cannot be to protect investments made in violation of the laws of the host State or investments not made in good faith, obtained for example through misrepresentations, concealments or corruption, or amounting to an abuse of the international ICSID arbitration system. In other words, the purpose of international protection is to protect legal and *bona fide* investments."[348] The *Phoenix Action* tribunal thus held that "illegal investments" are not protected through ICSID arbitration, and that "this condition—the conformity of the establishment of the investment with the national laws—is implicit even when not expressly stated in the relevant BIT."[349]
- The ICSID tribunal in *Hamester v. Ghana* remarked: "An investment will not be protected if it has been created in violation of national or international principles of good faith; by way of corruption, fraud, or deceitful conduct; or if its creation itself constitutes a misuse of the system of international investment protection under the ICSID Convention. It will also not be protected if it is made in violation of the host State's law (as elaborated, *e.g.*

345 *Id.* ¶ 135.

346 *Id.* ¶¶ 143–144.

347 *Id.* ¶¶ 146, 325(3).

348 *Phoenix Action, Ltd. v. The Czech Republic*, ICSID Case No. ARB/06/5, Award dated Apr. 15, 2009 ¶ 100.

349 *Id.* ¶ 101 (finding that its position "has also been adopted in the case of *Plama*"); *id.* ¶ 106 (finding that "States cannot be deemed to offer access to the ICSID dispute settlement mechanism to investments not made in good faith").

by the tribunal in *Phoenix*)."[350] The *Hamester* tribunal concluded that these general principles "exist independently of specific language to this effect in the Treaty."[351]

- The ICSID tribunal in *SAUR v. Argentina* observed that the system of investment arbitration protects only lawful and bona fide systems: "Whether or not the BIT between France and Argentina mentions the requirement that the investor act in conformity with domestic legislation does not constitute a relevant factor. The condition of not committing a serious violation of the legal order is a tacit condition, inherent to any BIT as, in any event, it is incomprehensible that a State offer the benefit of protection through arbitration if the investor, in order to obtain such protection, has acted contrary to the law."[352]
- The tribunal in *Khan Resources v. Mongolia*, an ad hoc arbitration under the UNCITRAL arbitration rules brought under the ECT, held that "[a]n investor who has obtained its investment in the host state only by acting in bad faith or in violation of the laws of the host state, has brought him or herself within the scope of application of the ECT only as a result of his wrongful acts. Such an investor should not be allowed to benefit as a result, in accordance with the maxim *nemo auditur propriam turpitudinem allegans*."[353]
- The tribunal in *Minotte v. Poland*, an ICSID additional facility proceeding, noted that the claims arose out of the U.S.-Poland BIT, which did not expressly require that the investment be made in accordance with the host State's law.[354] Nonetheless, as the tribunal explained, "it is now generally accepted that investments made on the basis of fraudulent conduct cannot benefit from BIT protection; and this is a principle that is independent of

350 *Gustav FW Hamester GmbH & Co. KG v. Republic of Ghana*, ICSID Case No. ARB/07/24, Award dated June 18, 2010 ("*Hamester v. Ghana*") ¶ 123.

351 *Id.* ¶ 124.

352 *SAUR International S.A. v. Republic of Argentina*, ICSID Case No. ARB/04/4, Decision on Jurisdiction and Liability dated June 6, 2012 (translation) ("*Le fait que l'APRI entre la France et l'Argentine mentionne ou non l'exigence que l'investisseur agisse conformément à la législation interne ne constitue pas un facteur pertinent. La condition de ne pas commettre de violation grave de l'ordre juridique est une condition tacite, propre à tout APRI, car en tout état de cause, il est incompréhensible qu'un État offre le bénéfice de la protection par un arbitrage d'investissement si l'investisseur, pour obtenir cette protection, a agi à l'encontre du droit.*").

353 *Khan Resources Inc., Khan Resources B.V. and CAUC Holding Company Ltd. v. Government of Mongolia*, UNCITRAL, Decision on Jurisdiction dated July 25, 2012 ("*Khan Resources v. Mongolia*") ¶ 383.

354 *David Minnotte and Robert Lewis v. Republic of Poland*, ICSID Case No. ARB(AF)/10/1, Award dated May 16, 2014 ¶ 131.

the effect of any express requirement in a BIT that the investment be made in accordance with the host State's law."[355]

- The tribunal in *Yukos v. Russia*, an arbitration administered by the PCA and arising under the ECT, agreed that an investment made in violation of the host State's law or the principle of good faith will not be protected, irrespective of the specific text of the treaty.[356] The tribunal held that the purpose of investment treaties is "to encourage legal and *bona fide* investments," and, consequently, that "[a]n investor who has obtained an investment in the host State only by acting in bad faith or in violation of the laws of the host state ... should not be allowed to benefit from the Treaty."[357]
- The ICSID tribunal in the resubmitted *Fraport v. Philippines* arbitration noted that, "even absent the sort of explicit legality requirement" contained in the Germany-Philippine BIT in that case, "there is an increasingly well-established international principle which makes international legal remedies unavailable with respect to illegal investments, at least when such illegality goes to the essence of the investment."[358]
- The ICSID tribunal in *Blusun v. Italy* acknowledged that the ECT underlying the claims in that case "does not lay down an explicit requirement of legality," but that the ECT nonetheless did not protect "investments which are actually unlawful under the law of the host state at the time they were made because protection of such investments would be contrary to the international public order. This conclusion is consistent with numerous other decisions and awards."[359]
- The ICSID tribunal in *Cortec Mining v. Kenya* remarked that "[i]t is accepted jurisprudence that in order to be protected an investment has to be in accordance with the laws of the host State and made in good faith."[360]

355 *Id.*

356 *Yukos Universal Limited (Isle of Man) v. The Russian Federation*, PCA Case No. AA 227, Final Award dated July 18, 2014 ("*Yukos v. Russia*") ¶¶ 1351–1352. The *Yukos* award was set aside on an unrelated ground. White & Case LLP represents the Russian Federation in the set aside and enforcement proceedings.

357 *Id.* ¶ 1352.

358 *Fraport v. Philippines II* ¶ 332; *id.* ¶ 328 ("Investment treaty cases confirm that such treaties do not afford protection to illegal investments either based on clauses of the treaties, as in the present case according to the above analysis, or, absent an express provision in the treaty, based on rules of international law, such as the 'clean hands' doctrine or doctrines to the same effect.").

359 *Blusun S.A., Jean-Pierre Lecorcier and Michael Stein v. Italian Republic*, ICSID Case No. ARB/14/3, Award dated Dec. 27, 2016 ¶ 264.

360 *Cortec Mining Kenya Limited et al. v. Republic of Kenya*, ICSID Case No. ARB/15/29, Award dated Oct. 22, 2018 ¶ 260; *id.* ¶ 321 (holding that "for an investment to be protected on

These cases reflect the majority view. Several tribunals, however, have disagreed with the notion of an implicit legality requirement. Thus, in contrast to the decisions in *Plama, Yukos*, and *Blusun* finding that the ECT protects only investments made in compliance with law, the tribunals in both *Liman v. Kazakhstan* and *Stati v. Kazakhstan* concluded that the ECT does not impose any legality requirement. As the *Stati* tribunal explained, "if the contracting states had intended there to be such a requirement, they could have written it into the text of the Treaty," particularly "in view of the extremely detailed definition of investment and other details regulated in the ECT."[361]

The ICSID tribunal in *Saba Fakes v. Turkey* similarly held that the State parties to investment treaties "are at liberty to condition their application and the whole protection they afford, including consent to arbitration, to a legality requirement of one form or another."[362] The *Saba Fakes* tribunal concluded, however, that a legality requirement or principles of good faith could not be imported into the definition of investment in the ICSID Convention "without doing violence" to the text of the Convention, and that "an investment might be 'legal' or 'illegal,' made in 'good faith' or not," but that "it nonetheless remains an investment."[363]

And, while the Israel-Uzbekistan BIT underlying the claims in *Metal-Tech* contained an express legality requirement, the tribunal in that case rejected the view that compliance with the laws of the host State and with the principle of good faith are elements of an objective definition of investment in the ICSID Convention.[364]

---

the international level, it has to be in substantial compliance with the significant legal requirement of the host state").

361 *Anatolie Stati, Gabriel Stati, Ascom Group S.A. and Terra Raf Trans Traiding Ltd v. Republic of Kazakhstan*, SCC Case No. V116/2010, Award dated Dec. 19, 2013 ¶ 812. *See also Liman v. Kazakhstan* ¶ 187 (concluding that the scope of Kazakhstan's consent to jurisdiction "must be understood to extend also to those investments in respect of which the underlying transaction was made in breach of Kazakh law and was therefore voidable," and that, consequently, even if the investment were found to have been made in violation of Kazakh law, "the question of legality might be relevant to the merits, but it would not have preclusive effect at the level of jurisdiction").

362 *Saba Fakes v. Turkey* ¶ 114.

363 *Id.* ¶ 112 (further observing that "[t]he expressions 'legal investment' or 'investment made in good faith' are not pleonasms, and the expressions 'illegal investment' or 'investment made in bad faith' are not oxymorons").

364 *Metal-Tech v. Uzbekistan* ¶¶ 126–127 (observing that State parties to an investment treaty "may limit the protections of the treaty to investments made in accordance with the laws and regulations of the host State," which, depending on the wording, may be a bar to jurisdiction or a defense on the merits, but that "does not mean that these elements are

Notwithstanding this divergence of views as to whether there is an implicit legality requirement in the ICSID Convention or investment treaties more generally, it is highly doubtful that any tribunal would admit claims arising out of an investment made through corruption (as opposed to a lesser violation of law), irrespective of the terms of the underlying treaty. Article V(2)(b) of the New York Convention and Articles 34(2)(b)(ii) and 36(1)(ii) of the UNCITRAL Model Law both provide that courts may refuse to enforce an arbitral award that is contrary to public policy,[365] and it is well established that corruption is contrary to international public policy.[366]

Moreover, while the contracting States to the ICSID Convention have undertaken to recognize and enforce any ICSID award as if it were a final judgment of their own court,[367] international tribunals themselves have an obligation to ensure that their awards accord with public policy. Thus, while the *Liman* tribunal disagreed with the view that investment treaties such as the ECT contain an implicit legality requirement, it agreed that it would "not have jurisdiction over investments made in violation of international public policy," including where the investment was made through fraud or bribery.[368] The tribunal in *Kim v. Uzbekistan* similarly confirmed that the international public policy against corruption "is present implicitly in BITs," and that the claims therefore would be inadmissible "where the investment at issue was made possible by such corruption."[369]

These public policy considerations effectively nullified an award of over US$ 200 million in the ICSID case of *Siemens v. Argentina*. After Siemens prevailed in that arbitration, one of its senior executives testified in German court that Siemens had paid bribes to make its investment. Argentina thus filed a request for the tribunal to revise its award in light of this new testimony.[370] While that request was still pending, Siemens and its Argentine subsidiary pleaded guilty to violating provisions of the FCPA and agreed to pay fines and penalties to the U.S. and German authorities totaling more than

part of the objective definition of the term 'investment' contained in Article 25(1) of the ICSID Convention").

365 Convention on the Recognition and Enforcement of Foreign Arbitral Awards (the "New York Convention") (1958) Article V(2)(b); UNCITRAL Model Law on International Commercial Arbitration ("UNCITRAL Model Law") (1985, amended in 2006) Articles 34(2)(b)(ii) and 36(1)(ii).

366 *See supra* § 2.

367 ICSID Convention Art. 54.

368 *Liman v. Kazakhstan* ¶ 194.

369 *Kim v. Uzbekistan* ¶ 593.

370 Luke E. Peterson, "Argentina and Siemens Ask Annulment Panel to Suspend Proceedings, So Original Arbitrators Can Look at Bribes Evidence," IA Reporter, July 28, 2008.

US$ 1.6 billion.[371] Siemens also agreed to a Statement of Offense stating that it had paid over US$ 100 million to a consulting group that "provided no legitimate services on the project" and to other entities with the understanding that "some or all of those funds would be passed along to Argentine officials for the corrupt purpose of obtaining, retaining, or reinstating" its project.[372] In light of these admissions, and as part of its settlement with the U.S. and German authorities, Siemens withdrew its arbitration claims and agreed to forego enforcement of the award.[373]

In sum, tribunals and courts will not give effect to investments made through corruption, irrespective of the specific treaty underlying the claims.

### 6.4 *Post-investment Corruption May Have Consequences for the Merits or Quantum of the Claims*

There is an important temporal limitation to illegality defenses in investment arbitration. In order to deprive an investor of treaty protection, the illegality must have occurred during the making of the investment. Post-investment corruption, fraud, or illegality may have consequences for the merits of the claims or the amount of compensation awarded, but will not result in a lack of jurisdiction or in the inadmissibility of the claims.

Tribunals in several cases have rejected arguments by States that the applicable treaty required that the investment not only be made in accordance with law, but that it be operated lawfully too. For example, in *Metal-Tech*, the Israel-Uzbekistan BIT defined "investments" as "any kind of assets, implemented in accordance with the laws and regulations of the Contracting Party in whose territory the investment is made."[374] While the tribunal agreed with Uzbekistan that "implemented" could mean "made, carried out, operated,

371 *United States v. Siemens Aktiengesellschaft*, District Court for the District of Columbia, Criminal Case No. CR-08-367-RJL, Plea Agreement Letter dated Dec. 15, 2008. *See also* U.S. Securities and Exchange Commission, "SEC Charges Siemens AG for Engaging in Worldwide Bribery," Dec. 15, 2008 (reporting that Siemens had agreed to pay US$ 350 million in disgorgement to the U.S. Securities and Exchange Commission, a US$ 450 million fine to the U.S. Department of Justice, and fines of US$ 854 million to the Office of the Prosecutor General in Munich).

372 *United States of America v. Siemens S.A. (Argentina)*, District Court for the District of Columbia, Criminal Case No. 08-368-RJL, Statement of Offense dated Dec. 15, 2008 ¶¶ 20–24.

373 U.S. Department of Justice Office of Public Affairs, "Former Siemens Executive Pleads Guilty to Role in $100 Million Foreign Bribery Scheme," Mar. 15, 2018 (reporting that in August 2009 "Siemens AG withdrew its claim to the more than $200 million arbitration award").

374 *Metal-Tech v. Uzbekistan* ¶ 164.

completed, performed, carried out into effect," the tribunal concluded that, in the context of the BIT, "the term 'assets implemented' refers to the time when the investment was made."[375] The *Metal-Tech* tribunal therefore held that the BIT required the investor to make its initial investment lawfully and did not address whether it must also operate in accordance with law after its investment had been made.[376]

The tribunal in the first *Fraport* arbitration similarly disagreed with the Philippines that the Germany-Philippines BIT required the investment to be both made and continuously operated in accordance with law.[377] The tribunal held that the BIT's legality requirement was "limited to the initiation of the investment," and that, if the investment was made lawfully, alleged violations of law in operating the investment "might be a defense to claimed *substantive* violations of the BIT, but could not deprive a tribunal acting under the authority of the BIT of its jurisdiction."[378] The second tribunal interpreted the BIT in the same way.[379]

The *Hamester* tribunal likewise held that the Germany-Ghana BIT underlying the claims in that case was limited temporally to requiring legality in making the investment, whereas illegality in operating the investment would not bear on jurisdiction although "it may well be relevant in the context of the substantive merits of a claim brought under the BIT."[380] While the tribunal further held that compliance with law in making the investment was required by general principles of international law irrespective of the specific language in the treaty (as discussed above), the tribunal emphasized that these general principles did not expand the temporal scope of the legality requirement.[381] The tribunal accordingly decided that, for purposes of jurisdiction, it was "only concerned with allegations of fraud in the initiation of the investment, and not with the multiple allegations of fraudulent conduct during the life of the investment."[382]

---

375 *Id.* ¶¶ 187, 193.

376 *Id.* ¶ 193.

377 *Fraport v. Philippines I* ¶¶ 344–345.

378 *Id.* ¶ 345.

379 *Fraport v. Philippines II* ¶ 333 (concluding that the BIT "requires that an investment comply with the laws of the host State at the time it is made in order to be accorded protection under the BIT," and that the tribunal's assessment of the alleged illegality "will therefore focus on the time of entry of Claimant's investment").

380 *Hamester v. Ghana* ¶ 127.

381 *Id.*

382 *Id.* ¶ 129; *id.* ¶ 128 (finding that "the award in *Fraport v. Philippines* was particularly clear on this distinction").

Other tribunals also have emphasized this temporal distinction. As the tribunals in *Khan Resources* and *Yukos* both explained, the State may regulate the activities of individuals and entities operating in its own jurisdiction in accordance with its own laws, and there thus is "no compelling reason" to deny altogether the right to invoke treaty protection to an investor that made a lawful investment but breached a local law during its subsequent operations:

> If the investor acts illegally, the host state can impose upon it sanctions available under local law.... However, if the investor believes these sanctions to be unjustified, it must have the possibility of challenging their validity. It would undermine the purpose and object of the Treaty to deny the investor the right to make its case before an arbitral tribunal based on the same alleged violations the existence of which the investor seeks to dispute on the merits.[383]

Moreover, in the specific context of corruption, a prospective investor confronted with a bribe demand at the outset has both the ability and the obligation to "walk away" and refuse to make such an illegal investment. Once an investor has made a significant investment, however, there is a much greater risk that State officials may coercively threaten to retaliate against or even expropriate the investment unless the investor pays a bribe. Where a bribe is paid during the course of operations, there may be a dispute about the validity of any State measures taken to prosecute the corrupt parties and what, if any, financial effect the corruption had on the value of the investment (e.g., if it facilitated tax evasion or other illegal activities that unjustly enriched the investor at the State's expense). For these reasons, illegality in operating the investment may be relevant to the merits of the claims or to the amount of compensation awarded, but likely would not result in a lack of jurisdiction or in the inadmissibility of the claims.[384]

383 *Khan Resources v. Mongolia* ¶ 384. *See also Yukos v. Russian Federation* ¶ 1355.

384 *See, e.g., Oxus Gold v. The Republic of Uzbekistan*, UNCITRAL, Final Award dated Dec. 17, 2015 ¶¶ 707, 709 (holding that BIT protection would be lost only if "the illegality affects the 'making', i.e. arises when initiating the investment itself and not just when implementing and/or operating it," and that unlawful operations thus "are irrelevant for the issue of jurisdiction or admissibility" but "may nevertheless be relevant when assessing the justifiable character of certain of Respondent's actions ... or as an element of the evaluation of damages"); *Khan Resources v. Mongolia* ¶¶ 384–385; *Yukos v. Russian Federation* ¶¶ 1354–1356. White & Case LLP represented the Republic of Uzbekistan in *Oxus Gold v. Uzbekistan*.

## VII Objections Based on Attribution and Estoppel Where the State Does Not Prosecute the Alleged Corruption

Now that several cases have been dismissed on corruption grounds, commentators have raised issues of attribution and estoppel to argue that a State should not be immunized from its wrongful conduct in corruption cases. We address these arguments below.

First, with regard to attribution, the objection is that bribery "takes two to tango." Thus, according to one commentator, bribery is a "bilateral" act that, by its nature, involves the participation of both the investor and a State official, and it would be unfair and may even create "perverse incentives" to allow the State to raise corruption as a defense, because "the more corrupt the state's officials, the less liable the state becomes."[385]

This argument does not accord with the rules on state responsibility under international law reflected in the U.N. International Law Commission ("ILC") Articles on the Responsibility of States for Internationally Wrongful Acts. ILC Article 7 provides: "The conduct of an organ of a State or of a person or entity empowered to exercise elements of the governmental authority shall be considered an act of the State under international law if the organ, person or entity acts in that capacity, even if it exceeds its authority or contravenes instructions."[386] The commentary to ILC Article 7 clarifies that a State official's *ultra vires* conduct thus is considered an act of the State under international law if the official acted in his or her official capacity, but that such conduct is not attributable to the State if the official acted in his or her private capacity:

> Cases where officials acted in their capacity as such, albeit unlawfully or contrary to instructions, must be distinguished from cases where the conduct is so removed from the scope of their official functions that it should be assimilated to that of private individuals, not attributable to the State. In the words of the Iran-United States Claims Tribunal, the

385 Aloysius P. Llamzon, "On Corruption's Peremptory Treatment in International Arbitration: State Responsibility, Unclean Hands, and the Return of Corruption as a Jurisdictional Issue," *in* ADDRESSING ISSUES OF CORRUPTION IN COMMERCIAL INVESTMENT ARBITRATION 35–37 (International Chamber of Commerce ed., 2014). *See also, e.g.*, Bernardo Cremades, "Corruption in Investment Arbitration," *in* GLOBAL REFLECTIONS ON INTERNATIONAL LAW, COMMERCE AND DISPUTE RESOLUTION: LIBER AMICORUM ROBERT BRINER, Gerald Aksen (ed.), 2005 at 216.

386 Draft Articles on Responsibility of States for Internationally Wrongful Acts (Nov. 2001) Art. 7.

> question is whether the conduct has been 'carried out by persons cloaked with governmental authority'.[387]

The commentary further provides that, in determining whether an official acted within his or her official capacity, even if unauthorized, "the question is whether they were acting with apparent authority."[388] In corruption cases, however, the bribing party would have no basis to contend that the corrupt official's acceptance of the bribe was done with apparent authority or cloaked with governmental authority, but instead would know that the official was subverting the State's interests for his or her own personal and illicit benefit. Accordingly, while the official acts of a corrupt official (e.g., a court judgment or government approval procured through corruption) may be attributable to the State, particularly in relation to third parties, the commentary to ILC Article 7 confirms that a corrupt official's conduct vis-à-vis the bribing party is private action that is not attributable to the State.[389]

The ILC's special rapporteur on state responsibility, Judge James Crawford, also confirmed in his treatise on state responsibility that "a state is not responsible for every act done by an individual in its service, but only when the individual purports to act on behalf of the state. Where an individual does something in his or her capacity as a private citizen, state responsibility will not arise."[390] Judge Crawford thus distinguished between an *ultra vires* act that would give rise to State responsibility and "a strictly private act" that would not, and as an example of the latter he referred to the Iran-U.S. Claims Tribunal's decision in *Yeager v. Iran*.[391] In that case, as Judge Crawford explained, the tribunal did not hold Iran responsible for the solicitation of a bribe by an agent of Iran Air who was indirectly a State employee, observing:

> Acts which an organ commits in a purely private capacity, even if it has used the means placed at its disposal by the State for the exercise of its function, are not attributable to the State ... The critical question here,

387 ILC Commentary to the Articles on Responsibility of States for Internationally Wrongful Acts (2001), Chapter II, Art. 7 at 46.

388 *Id.*

389 *Id.* at 46 fn. 150 ("The question of the responsibility of the State whose official had been bribed towards the corrupting State in such a case could hardly arise, but there could be issues of its responsibility towards a third party, which would be properly resolved under article 7.").

390 James Crawford, STATE RESPONSIBILITY: THE GENERAL PART, Cambridge University Press (2013) at 137.

391 *Id.* at 137–138.

> then, is whether the Iran Air agent was acting in his official capacity as an organ of Iran Air when he demanded the extra payment. There is no indication in this case that the Iran Air agent was acting for any other reason than personal profit, or that he had passed on the payment to Iran Air. He evidently did not act on behalf or in the interests of Iran Air. The Tribunal finds, therefore, that this agent acted in a private capacity and not in his official capacity as an organ for Iran Air.[392]

These observations will apply in almost any corruption case, as corrupt officials do not act in the interests of the State or pass along their bribes to the State. The ICSID tribunal in *World Duty Free* thus concluded that Kenya had not known about the bribe paid to the President of Kenya until the arbitration proceedings and thus could not have affirmed the bribe or waived any of its rights, and, further, that "there can be no affirmation or waiver in this case based on the knowledge of the Kenyan President attributable to Kenya."[393] On the contrary, as the tribunal explained, the payment "was a covert bribe; and accordingly its receipt is not legally to be imputed to Kenya itself. If it were otherwise, the payment would not be a bribe."[394]

Second and relatedly, commentators have argued that a State should be estopped from raising corruption or other illegality as a defense if it failed to prosecute the alleged wrongdoers in its domestic courts.[395] Estoppel is a general principle of international law that has three requirements: (i) a clear and unambiguous statement of fact; (ii) that was voluntary, unconditional, and authorized; and (iii) was relied on in good faith "either to the detriment of the party so relying on the statement or to the advantage of the party making the statement."[396] The quintessential requirement is "conduct which causes

392 *Id.* at 138 (quoting *Yeager v. Islamic Republic of Iran* (1987) 17 Iran—US CTR 92 at 111).

393 *World Duty Free v. Kenya* ¶¶ 184–185.

394 *Id.* ¶ 169; *id.* ¶ 185. While World Duty Free argued that President Moi was "one of the remaining 'Big Men' of Africa, who, under the one-party State Constitution was entitled to say, like Louis XIV, he *was* the State,'" the *World Duty Free* tribunal rejected this argument as "ill-founded." *Id.*

395 *See, e.g.*, Nassib G. Ziadé, "Accountability for Corruption in Investment Arbitration: Equitable Remedies for Findings of Illegality," *in* BCDR INTERNATIONAL ARBITRATION REVIEW, Kluwer Law International 2016, Volume 3, Issue 2, Nassib G. Ziadé (ed) at 436–437; Kevin Lim, "Upholding Corrupt Investors' Claims against Complicit or Compliant Host States—Where Angels Should Not Fear to Tread," Yearbook on International Investment Law and Policy 2011–2012 (2013) ¶ 66.

396 *Pope & Talbot Inc. v. Government of Canada*, NAFTA, UNCITRAL, Interim Award dated June 26, 2000 ("*Pope & Talbot*"), ¶ 111. *See also, e.g.*, *Pan American v. Argentina*, ICSID Case No. ARB/04/8, Decision on Preliminary Objections dated July 27, 2006 ¶ 151.

the other party, in reliance on such conduct, detrimentally to change its position or to suffer some prejudice."[397]

A leading case on estoppel is *Desert Line v. Yemen*, where the ICSID tribunal stated:

> Addressing the precise issue of estoppel, the ICSID tribunal in *Fraport* wrote (at para. 346): 'Principles of fairness should require a tribunal to hold a government estopped from raising violations of its own law as a jurisdictional defense when it knowingly overlooked them and endorsed an investment which was not in compliance with its law.'[398]

While these remarks are frequently quoted, *Desert Line* is inapposite in the context of alleged illegality. In fact, the tribunal observed in the next sentence that the alleged problem with Desert Line's investment was "not violation of law, but merely ... the failure to accomplish a formality foreseen by law, and not even required by it except as a condition of obtaining benefits unconnected with those of the BIT itself."[399] As the tribunal explained, Desert Line had invested hundreds of millions of dollars in a project with considerable risks to achieve objectives of national strategic importance, and was accused of nothing more than allegedly failing to obtain "some unspecified stamped or signed form from a governmental subdivision."[400] The tribunal also noted that the Prime Minister and other State authorities had made "unambiguous" written statements approving the investment, and that Desert Line's "detrimental reliance on the assurances from the highest organs" of the State was "obvious and indeed uncontradicted."[401] In these circumstances, the *Desert Line* tribunal therefore had "no hesitation" in holding that Yemen was estopped from raising formalistic arguments to contest jurisdiction.[402]

In *Fraport*, as discussed above, two ICSID tribunals both determined that they lacked jurisdiction because Fraport had made its investment in violation of the Philippine anti-dummy law.[403] With regard to the lack of prosecution, the tribunal in the first *Fraport* arbitration noted that even if the Philippine

---

397 *Pope & Talbot* ¶ 111; IAN BROWNLIE, PRINCIPLES OF PUBLIC INTERNATIONAL LAW 420, 8th ed., Oxford University Press, 2012.

398 *Desert Line Projects LLC v. The Republic of Yemen*, ICSID Case No. ARB/05/17, Award dated Feb. 6, 2008 ("*Desert Line v. Yemen*") ¶ 120; *Fraport v. Philippines I* ¶ 346.

399 *Id.* ¶ 120.

400 *Desert Line v. Yemen* ¶ 119.

401 *Id.* ¶¶ 118–119.

402 *Id.* ¶ 118.

403 *See supra* § 6.3.

prosecutor had directly dealt with the "secret shareholder agreements" establishing the illegality, its findings "would not constitute a *res judicata* because of a difference in the identity of the parties and the claim."[404] The tribunal further explained that it also could not be bound by a decision of the Philippine courts on this issue either:

> [H]oldings of municipal legal institutions cannot be binding with respect to matters properly within the jurisdiction of this Tribunal. As the *Inceysa* tribunal put it, 'as the legality of the investment is a premise for this Tribunal's jurisdiction, the determination of such legality can only be made by the tribunal hearing the case, i.e. by this Arbitral Tribunal'.[405]

The tribunal nonetheless agreed with Fraport that, while not binding, a failure to prosecute alleged illegality, "such that an investor reasonably inferred that it was acting lawfully and made further investments, could obviate an objection to jurisdiction *ratione materiae*."[406] The tribunal found, however, that Fraport "consciously concealed" its illegality, "such that any actions that might otherwise have been viewed by a foreign investor in good faith as endorsements by the Philippine government cannot be deemed to have cured the violation or estopped the Government."[407] The tribunal therefore rejected Fraport's estoppel arguments, observing that "a covert arrangement, which by its nature is unknown to the government officials who may have given approbation to the project, cannot be any basis for estoppel," as "the covert character of the arrangement would deprive any legal validity (assuming that informal and possibly *contra legem* endorsements would have legal validity under the relevant law) that an expression of approbation or an endorsement might otherwise have had."[408]

As with the illegality in *Fraport*, corruption is by its nature covert. Corruption also violates international public policy and the laws of nearly all, if not all,

404 *Fraport v. Philippines I* ¶ 390.

405 *Id.* ¶ 391.

406 *Id.* ¶ 387.

407 *Id.* (finding that the Philippines "could hardly have initiated legal action against [Fraport] for violations which [Fraport] had concealed"); *id.* ¶ 347 (finding "no indication in the record that the Republic of the Philippines knew, should have known or could have known of the covert arrangements which were not in accordance with Philippine law when Fraport first made its investment in 1999").

408 *Id.* Seven years later, following the annulment of the first *Fraport* award, the tribunal in the second arbitration similarly rejected Fraport's estoppel arguments and refused jurisdiction even though the Philippines still had not prosecuted anyone for the illegality. *Fraport v. Philippines II* ¶¶ 467–469.

States. Thus, where an investor had made its investment by paying a covert bribe, any statement about the alleged legality of its investment would either be misinformed as to the existence of the bribe (and therefore not clear and unambiguous) or unauthorized.

Prosecutors also have considerable discretion in deciding whether to bring criminal charges. It therefore may be going too far, at least in some cases, to infer a State's acquiescence in corruption from its decision not to prosecute. Moreover, even if such an inference could be drawn, an inference is not a clear and unambiguous statement of fact.

In any event, an investor that knowingly had paid a bribe could not reasonably rely in good faith to its detriment on any affirmation as to the alleged legality of its investment, nor on the lack of prosecution as evidencing such alleged legality. For these reasons, the doctrine of estoppel would not normally bar a State from raising a corruption defense.[409] Indeed, to the authors' knowledge, no tribunal in an investment arbitration has estopped a State from raising a corruption defense due to its failure to bring criminal charges in its domestic courts.

Furthermore, in the three investment arbitrations dismissed specifically on grounds of corruption—*World Duty Free, Metal-Tech*, and *Spentex*—the ICSID tribunals dismissed the claims in their entirety even though none of the investors or State officials in those cases was prosecuted for corruption. The *World Duty Free* tribunal commented in this respect:

> It remains nonetheless a highly disturbing feature in this case that the corrupt recipient of [World Duty Free's] bribe was more than an officer of state but its most senior officer, the Kenyan President, and that it is Kenya which is here advancing as a complete defence to [World Duty Free's] claims the illegalities of its own former President. Moreover, on the evidence before this Tribunal, the bribe was apparently solicited by the Kenyan President and not wholly initiated by [World Duty Free]. Although the Kenyan President has now left office and is no longer immune from suit under the Kenyan Constitution, it appears that no attempt has been made by Kenya to prosecute him for corruption or to recover the bribe in civil proceedings. It is not therefore surprising

409 Brody Greenwald, "The Viability of Corruption Defenses in Investment Arbitration When the State Does Not Prosecute," Blog of the European Journal of International Law dated Apr. 15, 2015, available at https://www.ejiltalk.org/the-viability-of-corruption-defenses-in-investment-arbitration-when-the-state-does-not-prosecute/ (last accessed Apr. 15, 2019).

> that Mr. Ali feels strongly the unfairness of the legal case now advanced by Kenya….[410]

As the *World Duty Free* tribunal explained, however, similar complaints of unfairness were "voiced centuries ago" by earlier litigants and were "fully answered" on the ground that, as regards public policy, "the law protects not the litigating parties but the public; or in this case, the mass of tax-payers and other citizens making up one of the poorest countries in the world."[411] Quoting Lord Mansfield, the tribunal further commented: "The general principle of public policy is this: *ex dolo malo non oritur actio*. No court will lend its aid to a man who founds his cause of action upon an immoral or illegal act."[412]

Similarly, in *Metal-Tech*, Metal-Tech complained that neither the Prime Minister nor his brother nor any other official was charged in connection with its project.[413] The *Metal-Tech* tribunal did not find this to be a relevant consideration. The tribunal also noted that, while it was "sensitive to the ongoing debate that findings of corruption often come down heavily on claimants" and may for that reason appear "unsatisfactory" and "unfair," the objective was "not to punish one party at the cost of the other, but rather to ensure the promotion of the rule of law, which entails that a court or tribunal cannot grant assistance to a party that has engaged in a corrupt act."[414]

According to published reports, the ICSID tribunal in *Spentex* also dismissed the claims even though the corrupt State officials were not investigated, prosecuted, or even identified.[415]

While the State thus will not be estopped from raising a corruption defense due to its failure to prosecute, there may be other consequences in the arbitration. The *World Duty Free* and *Metal-Tech* tribunals both refused to award costs to the States in those cases, and the *Metal-Tech* tribunal further determined that it lacked jurisdiction to consider Uzbekistan's counter-claims due to the

---

410 *World Duty Free v. Kenya* ¶ 180.

411 *Id.* ¶ 181.

412 *Id.* (quoting Lord Mansfield in *Holman v. Johnson* (1775) 1 Cowp. 341, 343).

413 *Metal-Tech v. Uzbekistan* ¶ 336.

414 *Id.* ¶ 389; *id.* ¶ 422 ("The law is clear—and rightly so—that in such a situation the investor is deprived of protection and, consequently, the host State avoids any potential liability."). *See also, e.g.*, ICC Case No. 6497 ¶ 2 ("The enterprise having benefited from the bribes (i.e., having obtained substantial contracts thanks to the bribes) has not a better moral position than the enterprise having organised the payment of the bribes. The nullity of the agreement is generally only beneficial to the former, and thus possibly inequitable. But this is legally irrelevant.").

415 Djanic, Newly Unearthed Ruling.

corruption.[416] Moreover, according to published reports, the *Spentex* tribunal, by majority, ordered Uzbekistan to pay US$ 8 million to an anticorruption fund of the United Nations Development Programme, failing which it would have to pay a substantial part of Spentex's legal costs.[417]

Several other tribunals indicated that the lack of prosecution reinforced and confirmed their findings that the transactions at issue were lawful and not corrupt. In *Wena Hotels v. Egypt*, for example, the ICSID tribunal observed that the Egyptian government had been aware of the consulting agreement allegedly used to conceal corrupt payments, "but decided (for whatever reasons) not to prosecute" the consultant, and, therefore, the tribunal was "reluctant to immunize Egypt from liability in this arbitration because it now alleges that the agreement … was illegal under Egyptian law."[418] The tribunal did not dismiss the allegations on that basis though. Rather, the tribunal found that Egypt largely had "failed to present any evidence that would refute Wena's evidence that the Contract was a legitimate agreement to help pursue development opportunities in Misr Aswan."[419]

In *Karkey v. Pakistan*, the ICSID tribunal criticized Pakistan for "asking the Tribunal to embark upon an investigation as to the existence of corruption" nearly three years into the proceedings, "after the Pakistani authorities, with powers considerably greater than those of the Tribunal, had failed to establish the existence of such corruption after several years of investigation."[420] The tribunal also found "no evidence of corruption on the record," and that Pakistan's "last minute allegations" were more likely aimed "at derailing the arbitration proceedings than at genuinely allowing corruption to be established."[421]

---

416 *World Duty Free v. Kenya* ¶¶ 190–192; *Metal-Tech v. Uzbekistan* ¶¶ 422, 423.

417 Luke Eric Peterson and Vladislav Djanic, "In an Innovative Award, Arbitrators Pressure Uzbekistan—Under Threat of Adverse Cost Order—to Donate to UN Anti-Corruption Initiative; Also Propose Future Treaty-Drafting Changes That Would Penalize States for Corruption," IA Reporter, June 22, 2017.

418 *Wena Hotels Ltd. v. Arab Republic of Egypt*, ICSID Case No. ARB/98/4, Award dated Dec. 8, 2000 ¶ 116 (noting that the relevant facts were passed to the prosecutor, but that it did "not know whether an investigation was conducted and, if so, whether the investigation was closed because the prosecutor determined that [the accused] was innocent, because of lack of evidence, or because of complicity by other government officials").

419 *Id.* ¶ 117.

420 *Karkey v. Pakistan* ¶ 537; *id.* ¶¶ 538–539 (finding it "important to note" that the Supreme Court of Pakistan made no specific finding of corruption in relation to Karkey, and that, after investigating allegations of corruption related to the Project for four years including through "a detailed examination of all accounts and documents," the Executive Agency tasked with the authority to investigate had "not found any evidence of corruption related to Karkey").

421 *Id.* ¶ 543.

The tribunal therefore concluded that, even on a balance of probabilities standard of proof, there was insufficient evidence that Karkey had engaged in corruption.[422]

And, in *Union Fenosa v. Egypt*, the ICSID tribunal observed that Egypt first raised allegations of corruption in the arbitration more than 15 years after the agreement in question was concluded, and that while the lapse of time, by itself, did not bar Egypt's defense under international law, it raised "doubts as to why such allegations were not raised and investigated by [Egypt's] criminal authorities long before … and why criminal prosecutions have still not been brought against certain individuals in Egypt."[423] As in *Wena Hotels* and *Karkey*, however, the case failed due to a lack of evidence, not a lack of prosecution. Specifically, the *Union Fenosa* tribunal found that Egypt had pointed out several "classic 'red flags'," but that "even the reddest of red flags does not suffice without proof of corruption before the tribunal."[424] The *Union Fenosa* tribunal concluded that, in a case of alleged corruption based on circumstantial evidence, "there have first to be dots in the evidence adduced before the tribunal," and in the majority's view there were "insufficient dots; and the red flags are outnumbered by neutral black flags."[425]

Accordingly, a State's failure to prosecute will not preclude it from raising a corruption defense in the arbitration, but may be taken into account by the tribunal in assessing the evidence of the alleged corruption and in awarding costs.

---

422 *Id.*

423 *Union Fenosa Gas* ¶ 7.53; *id.* ¶ 7.111 (observing that it was "significant" that a particular individual "was prosecuted and convicted for other crimes in Egypt," but not in connection with the alleged corrupt agreement, and that no Government official was prosecuted in regard to that agreement).

424 *Id.* ¶ 7.113.

425 *Id.* ¶ 7.114. One of the arbitrators dissented on the ground that the evidence was sufficient to meet Egypt's burden of proving corruption. *Id.* Dissenting Opinion of Mark Clodfelter dated Aug. 31, 2018 ¶¶ 5, 16 (finding "a tremendous and unexplained discrepancy" between the intermediary's involvement in the project and his compensation, which was "a clear red flag," and concluding that "the only inference that can be drawn is the one Claimant has sought to avoid, namely that [the intermediary's] high compensation was for the purpose of exerting improper influence upon government officials in allowing the project and awarding the SPA"). Egypt has filed an annulment application based largely on that dissenting opinion, which currently is pending. *See* Tom Jones, "Egypt Seeks to Annul Award Over Approach to Corruption 'Red Flags,'" Global Arbitration Review dated Jan. 11, 2019.

## VIII Conclusion

Corruption allegations are now routinely raised in international proceedings. These cases may have serious repercussions not only for the parties to the proceeding, but for other non-parties implicated in the alleged corruption. In view of the gravity of such allegations, tribunals generally require more compelling evidence to prove them. Where corruption is proven, the consequences typically will be decisive. Thus, a State that causes damage to an investor for refusing to pay a bribe will be held liable for violating its obligation to accord fair and equitable treatment, while claims founded on a contract or investment made through corruption will be dismissed.

While these consequences may seem unfair if the respondent is the State and no action has been taken to address the alleged corruption in its domestic courts, investors that make their initial investment by paying bribes have violated both host State law and international public policy. Such investors, therefore, have forfeited their right to seek justice before courts and tribunals and have no basis to complain about the consequences of their illicit activities.

## Bibliography

15 U.S. Code § 78dd.

A Resource Guide to the U.S. Foreign Corrupt Practices Act by the Criminal Division of the U.S. Department of Justice and the Enforcement Division of the U.S. Securities and Exchange Commission (2012).

*Adem Dogan v. Turkmenistan*, ICSID Case No. ARB/09/9, Decision on Annulment dated Jan. 15, 2016.

African Union Convention on Preventing and Combating Corruption, adopted July 1, 2003, entered into force Aug. 5, 2006.

*Alasdair Ross Anderson, et al. v. Republic of Costa Rica*, ICSID Case No. ARB(AF)/07/3, Award dated May 19, 2010.

*Alpha Projektholding GmbH v. Ukraine*, ICSID Case No. ARB/07/16, Award dated Nov. 8, 2010.

AMERICAN JURISPRUDENCE, 29 AM. JUR. 2D EVIDENCE (United States).

*Ampal-American Israel Corporation and others v. Arab Republic of Egypt*, ICSID Case No. ARB/12/11, Decision on Jurisdiction dated Feb. 1, 2016.

*Anatolie Stati, Gabriel Stati, Ascom Group S.A. and Terra Raf Trans Traiding Ltd v. Republic of Kazakhstan*, SCC Case No. V116/2010, Award dated Dec. 19, 2013.

Annual Report of the International Centre for the Settlement of Investment Disputes, Annual Report for 2017.

*Apotex Holdings Inc. and Apotex Inc. v. United States of America*, ICSID Case No. ARB(AF)12/1, Award dated Aug. 25, 2014.

*Arnaud Di Benedetto v. FIT*, CAS 2014/A/3519 & *Bastien Cotte-Barrot v. FIT*, CAS 2014/A/3520.

*Asian Agricultural Products Ltd. v. Republic of Sri Lanka*, ICSID Case No. ARB/87/3, Award dated June 27, 1990.

Australia Commercial Arbitration Act 2017.

*Azpetrol International Holdings B.V., Azpetrol Group B.V., and Azpetrol Oil Services Group B.V. v. Republic of Azerbaijan*, ICSID Case No. ARB/06/15, Award dated Sept. 8, 2009.

Baissus, Jean-Marc, "Common v. Continental: A Reaction to Mr. Evan Whitton's 1998 Murdoch Law School Address," 5 MURDOCH U. ELEC. J.L No. 4 (Dec. 1998).

*Bayindir Insaat Turizm Ve Sanayi A.S. v. Islamic Republic of Pakistan*, ICSID Case No. ARB/03/29, Award dated Aug. 27, 2009.

Bedrosyan, Alexander Sevan, "Adverse Inferences in International Arbitration," 38 U. PA. J. INT'L LAW 241.

*Bin Hammam v. Fédération Internationale de Football Association*, CAS 2011/A/2625, Award dated July 19, 2012.

*Blusun S.A., Jean-Pierre Lecorcier and Michael Stein v. Italian Republic*, ICSID Case No. ARB/14/3, Award dated Dec. 27, 2016.

Born, Gary, INTERNATIONAL COMMERCIAL ARBITRATION (2d ed., 2014).

*Briginshaw v. Briginshaw* (1938) 60 CLR 336.

Brownlie, Ian, PRINCIPLES OF PUBLIC INTERNATIONAL LAW, 8th ed., Oxford University Press, 2012.

Buisman, Caroline, Bouazdi, Myriam, and Costi, Matteo, "Principles of Civil Law," *in* PRINCIPLES OF EVIDENCE IN INTERNATIONAL CRIMINAL JUSTICE, Karim Khan, Caroline Buisman, and Christopher Gosnell eds., 2010.

Chatham House International Law Discussion Group Meeting, Mar. 28, 2007: "World Duty Free v. The Republic of Kenya: A Unique Precedent?".

Cheng, Bin, GENERAL PRINCIPLES OF LAW AS APPLIED BY INTERNATIONAL COURTS AND TRIBUNAL (1987).

*Chevron Corp. and Texaco Petroleum Co. v. The Republic of Ecuador*, PCA Case No. 2009-2003, UNCITRAL, Second Partial Award on Track II dated Aug. 30, 2018.

*Churchill Mining PLC and Planet Mining Pty Ltd v. Republic of Indonesia*, ICSID Cases Nos. ARB/12/14 and ARB/12/40, Award dated Dec. 6, 2016.

Clermont, Kevin and Sherwin, Emily, "A Comparative View of Standards of Proof," 50 AM. J. COMP. L. 243 (2002).

Clermont, Kevin, "Standards of Proof Revisited," 33 VERMONT LAW REV. 469 (2009).

*Commonwealth v. Wentzel*, 61 A.2d 309 (1948).

Convention on the Recognition and Enforcement of Foreign Arbitral Awards (1958).

*Cortec Mining Kenya Limited et al. v. Republic of Kenya*, ICSID Case No. ARB/15/29, Award dated Oct. 22, 2018.

Council of Europe Civil Law Convention on Corruption, ETS No. 174, opened for signature Nov. 4, 1999, entered into force Nov. 1, 2003.

Council of Europe Criminal Law Convention on Corruption, ETS No. 173, opened for signature Jan. 27, 1999, entered into force July 1, 2002.

Crawford, James, STATE RESPONSIBILITY: THE GENERAL PART, Cambridge University Press (2013).

Cremades, Bernardo, "Corruption in Investment Arbitration," *in* GLOBAL REFLECTIONS ON INTERNATIONAL LAW, COMMERCE AND DISPUTE RESOLUTION: LIBER AMICORUM ROBERT BRINER, Gerald Aksen (ed.), 2005.

*Dadras Int'l Islamic Republic of Iran*, Iran-U.S. Claims Tribunal, Award dated Nov. 7, 1995, Iran-U.S. Claims Tribunal Reports (2001).

*David Minnotte and Robert Lewis v. Republic of Poland*, ICSID Case No. ARB(AF)/10/1, Award dated May 16, 2014.

Davies, Dr. Chris, *The 'Comfortable Satisfaction Standard of Proof: Applied by the Court of Arbitration For Sport in Drug-Related Cases*, UNDALR (2002).

*Desert Line Projects LLC v. The Republic of Yemen*, ICSID Case No. ARB/05/17, Award dated Feb. 6, 2008.

Djanic, Vladislav, "In Newly Unearthed Uzbekistan Ruling, Exorbitant Fees Promised To Consultants On Eve Of Tender Process Are Viewed By Tribunal As Evidence Of Corruption, Leading To Dismissal Of All Claims Under Dutch BIT," IA Reporter, June 22, 2017.

*Doe and another v. Skegg and another*, EWHC 3746 (2006) (Ch).

Draft Articles on Responsibility of States for Internationally Wrongful Acts (Nov. 2001).

*ECE Projektmanagement International GmbH and Kommanditgesellschaft PANTA Achtundsechzigste Grundstücksgesellschaft mbH & Co v. Czech Republic*, PCA Case No. 2010-5, Award dated Sept. 19, 2013.

Economic Community of West African States Protocol on the Fight against Corruption, opened for signature Dec. 21, 2001, available at https://eos.cartercenter.org/uploads/document_file/path/406/ECOWAS_Protocol_on_Corruption.pdf (last accessed Apr. 15, 2019).

*EDF (Services) Limited v. Romania*, ICSID Case No. ARB/05/16, Award dated Oct. 8, 2009.

English Arbitration Act of 1996.

*Europe Cement Investment & Trade S.A. v. Republic of Turkey*, ICSID Case No. ARB(AF)/07/2, Award dated Aug. 13, 2009.

European Commission, Migration and Home Affairs, "Corruption," available at https://ec.europa.eu/home-affairs/what-we-do/policies/organized-crime-and-human-trafficking/corruption_en (last accessed Apr. 15, 2019).

European Union Convention against Corruption involving Officials, adopted May 26, 1997, entered into force Sept. 28, 2005, available at https://eur-lex.europa.eu/legal-content/EN/TXT/?uri=LEGISSUM:l33027 (last accessed Apr. 15, 2019).

*Evidence Act 1995* § 140 (Cth and NSW).

Explanatory Notes to UK Bribery Act of 2010.

*FC Metalist et. al. v. FFU*, CAS 2010/A/2267.

*FK Pobeda et al. v. UEFA*, CAS 2009/A/1920.

"Former Uzbek Government Official and Uzbek Telecommunications Executive Charged in Bribery and Money Laundering Scheme Involving the Payment of Nearly $1 Billion in Bribes," U.S. Department of Justice, U.S. Attorney's Office, Press Release dated Mar. 7, 2019.

*Fraport AG Frankfurt Airport Services Worldwide v. Republic of the Philippines*, ICSID Case No. ARB/11/12, Award dated Dec. 10, 2014.

*Fraport AG Frankfurt Airport Services Worldwide v. Republic of the Philippines*, ICSID Case No. ARB/03/25, Award dated Aug. 16, 2007.

*F-W Oil Interests, Inc. v. Republic of Trinidad & Tobago*, ICSID Case No. ARB/01/14, Award dated Mar. 3, 2006.

Geneva Code of Civil Procedure.

Greenwald, Brody K., "The Viability of Corruption Defenses in Investment Arbitration When the State Does Not Prosecute," Blog of the European Journal of International Law dated Apr. 15, 2015, available at https://www.ejiltalk.org/the-viability-of-corruption-defenses-in-investment-arbitration-when-the-state-does-not-prosecute/ (last accessed Apr. 15, 2019).

*Gustav FW Hamester GmbH & Co. KG v. Republic of Ghana*, ICSID Case No. ARB/07/24, Award dated June 18, 2010.

*H&H Enterprises Investments, Inc. v. Arab Republic of Egypt*, ICSID Case No. ARB/09/15, Excerpts of Award dated May 6, 2014.

Hwang, Michael and Lim, Kevin, "Corruption in Arbitration—Law and Reality," Asian International Arbitration Journal, Kluwer Law International 2012, Vol. 8, Issue 1.

ICC Award No. 3916 of 1982, Collection of ICC Arbitral Awards 1974–1985.

ICC Case No. 1110, Award of 1963, YCA 1996.

ICC Case No. 12990, Award dated Dec. 2005, *ICC Bulletin* (*Supplement*) 24 (2013).

ICC Case No. 13384, Award dated Dec. 2005, *ICC Bulletin* (*Supplement*) 24 (2013).

ICC Case No. 13515, Award dated Apr. 2006, *ICC Bulletin* (*Supplement*) 24 (2013).

ICC Case No. 13914, Final Award dated Mar. 2008, 24 *ICC Bulleting* (*Supplement*) 77 (2013).

ICC Case No. 3916, Award of 1982, *Collection of ICC Arbitral Awards 1974–1985* (Jarvin, Sigvard & Derains, Yves eds. 1990).

ICC Case No. 6497, Award of 1994, *Yearbook of Commercial Arbitration* 24a (1999).

ICC Case No. 8891, Award of 1998, *Journal du Droit International* 4 (2000).
ICC Commission on Corporate Responsibility and Anti-corruption, *ICC Guidelines on Agents, Intermediaries and Other Third Parties* (2010).
ICC International Corporate Integrity Handbook: Fighting Corruption (Fritz Heimann and Francois Vincke, eds., 2008).
ICSID Arbitration Rules.
ICSID Convention.
ILC Commentary to the Articles on Responsibility of States for Internationally Wrongful Acts (2001).
*In re Doherty* [2008] UKHL 33.
*In re Mobile TeleSystems PJSC*, File No. 3-19022, SEC, Order Instituting Cease-and-Desist Proceedings dated Mar. 6, 2019.
*Inceysa Vallisoletana, S.L. v. Republic of El Salvador*, ICSID Case No. ARB/03/26, Award dated Aug. 2, 2006.
Inter-American Convention Against Corruption (B-58), adopted Mar. 29, 1996, entered into force Mar. 6, 1997.
International Anti-Corruption Resource Center, Guide to Combatting Corruption & Fraud in Development Projects, available at https://guide.iacrc.org/potential-scheme-bribes-and-kickbacks/ (last accessed Apr. 15, 2019).
*Ioan Micula, Viorel Micula, SC European Food SA, SC Starmill SRL and SC Multipack SRL v. Romania*, ICSID Case No ARB/05/20, Decision on Jurisdiction and Admissibility dated Sept. 24, 2008.
*Ioannis Kardassopoulos and Ron Fuchs v. The Republic of Georgia*, ICSID Cases Nos. ARB/05/18 and ARB/07/15, Award dated Mar. 3, 2010.
Iran-United States Claims Tribunal Rules of Procedure dated 1983.
*Jan Oostergetel and Theodora Laurentius v. The Slovak Republic*, UNCITRAL, Final Award dated Apr. 23, 2012.
Jones, Tom, "Egypt Seeks to Annul Award Over Approach to Corruption 'Red Flags,'" Global Arbitration Review dated Jan. 11, 2019.
*Karkey Karadeniz Elektrik Uretim A.S. v. Islamic Republic of Pakistan*, ICSID Case No. ARB/13/1, Award dated Aug. 22, 2017.
*Kenya Airports Authority v. World Duty Free Co. Ltd.*, High Court of Kenya, Misc. Application No. 67 of 2013, Ruling dated Oct. 5, 2018.
*Khan Resources Inc., Khan Resources B.V. and CAUC Holding Company Ltd. v. Government of Mongolia*, UNCITRAL, Decision on Jurisdiction dated July 25, 2012.
Lamm, Carolyn B., Greenwald, Brody K., and Young, Kristen M., "From *World Duty Free* to *Metal-Tech*: A Review of International Investment Treaty Arbitration Cases Involving Allegations of Corruption," ICSID REVIEW, Vol. 29, No. 2 (2014).
*Libananco Holdings Co. Ltd. v. Republic of Turkey*, ICSID Case No. ARB/06/8, Award dated Sept. 2, 2011.

Lim, Kevin, "Upholding Corrupt Investors' Claims against Complicit or Compliant Host States—Where Angels Should Not Fear to Tread," Yearbook on International Investment Law and Policy 2011–2012 (2013).

*Liman Caspian Oil BV and NCL Dutch Investment BV v. Republic of Kazakhstan*, ICSID Case No. ARB/07/14, Excerpts of Award dated June 22, 2010.

Llamzon, Aloysius P. and Sinclair, Anthony, "Investor Wrongdoing in Investment Arbitration: Standards Governing Issues of Corruption, Fraud, Misrepresentation and Other Investor Misconduct," *in* Albert J. van den Berg, LEGITIMACY: MYTHS, REALITIES, CHALLENGES, 2015.

Llamzon, Aloysius P., "On Corruption's Peremptory Treatment in International Arbitration: State Responsibility, Unclean Hands, and the Return of Corruption as a Jurisdictional Issue," *in* ADDRESSING ISSUES OF CORRUPTION IN COMMERCIAL INVESTMENT ARBITRATION (International Chamber of Commerce ed., 2014).

Llamzon, Aloysius P., "State Responsibility for Corruption: The Attribution Asymmetry in International Investment Arbitration," Transnational Dispute Management, Vol. 10, Issue 3.

Malek, Hodge, Auburn, Jonathan, and Bagshaw, Roderick, PHIPSON ON EVIDENCE (17th ed. 2009).

*Marvin Roy Feldman Karpa v. United Mexican States*, ICSID Case No ARB(AF)/99/1, Award dated Dec. 16, 2002.

Mayanja, Sowed Juma, "Circumstantial Evidence and Its Admissibility in Criminal Proceedings: A Comparative Analysis of the Common Law and Islamic Law Systems," 67 J.L. POL'Y & GLOBALIZATION 26 (2017).

Menaker, Andrea J. and Greenwald, Brody K., "Proving Corruption in International Arbitration: Who Has the Burden and How Can it Be Met?," *in* ADDRESSING ISSUES OF CORRUPTION IN COMMERCIAL INVESTMENT ARBITRATION (International Chamber of Commerce ed., 2014).

*Metal-Tech Ltd. v. The Republic of Uzbekistan*, ICSID Case No. ARB/10/3, Award dated Oct. 4, 2013.

*Middle East Cement Shipping and Handling Co. S.A. v. Arab Republic of Egypt*, ICSID Case No. ARB/99/6, Award dated Apr. 12, 2002.

Moses, Margaret, THE PRINCIPLES AND PRACTICE OF INTERNATIONAL COMMERCIAL ARBITRATION (2nd ed. 2012).

Mourre, Alexis, "Arbitration in Criminal Law: Reflections on the Duties of the Arbitrator," Arbitration International 22:1 dated 2006.

*Mr. Saba Fakes v. Republic of Turkey*, ICSID Case No. ARB/07/20, Award dated July 14, 2010.

Muchlinski, Peter, Ortino, Federico and Schreuer, Christoph, THE OXFORD HANDBOOK OF INTERNATIONAL INVESTMENT LAW (2008), Oxford University Press.

*Neat Holdings Pty Ltd v. Karajan Holdings Pty Ltd.* (1992) 67 ALJR 170.

*Niko Resources (Bangladesh) Ltd. v. People's Republic of Bangladesh, Bangladesh Petroleum Exploration & Production Company Limited, and Bangladesh Oil Gas and Mineral Corporation*, ICSID Cases Nos. ARB/10/11 and ARB/10/18, Decision on Jurisdiction dated Aug. 19, 2013.

O'Malley, Nathan D., RULES OF EVIDENCE IN INTERNATIONAL ARBITRATION: AN ANNOTATED GUIDE (2012).

*Olympiakos Volou FC v. UEFA*, CAS 2011/A/2528.

Organisation for Economic Co-operation and Development Convention on Combating Bribery of Foreign Public Officials in International Business Transactions, adopted Dec. 17, 1997, entered into force Feb. 15, 1999.

*Oriekhov v. Union des Associations Européennes de Football (UEFA)*, CAS 2010/A/2172, Award dated Jan. 18, 2011.

*Oxus Gold v. The Republic of Uzbekistan*, UNCITRAL, Final Award dated Dec. 17, 2015.

*Pan American v. Argentina*, ICSID Case No. ARB/04/8, Decision on Preliminary Objections dated July 27, 2006.

Peterson, Luke E., "Argentina and Siemens Ask Annulment Panel to Suspend Proceedings, So Original Arbitrators Can Look at Bribes Evidence," IA Reporter, July 28, 2008.

Peterson, Luke Eric and Djanic, Vladislav, "In an Innovative Award, Arbitrators Pressure Uzbekistan—Under Threat of Adverse Cost Order—to Donate to UN Anti-Corruption Initiative; Also Propose Future Treaty-Drafting Changes That Would Penalize States for Corruption," IA Reporter, June 22, 2017.

*Phoenix Action, Ltd. v. The Czech Republic*, ICSID Case No. ARB/06/5, Award dated Apr. 15, 2009.

Pieth, Mark, "Contractual Freedom v. Public Policy Considerations in Arbitration," *in* PRIVATE LAW, NATIONAL-GLOBAL-COMPARATIVE, Büchler, Müller-Chen, (eds.), 2011.

*Plama Consortium Ltd. v. Republic of Bulgaria*, ICSID Case No. ARB/03/24, Award dated Aug. 27, 2008.

*Pope & Talbot Inc. v. Government of Canada*, NAFTA, UNCITRAL, Interim Award dated June 26, 2000.

*Pulp Mills (Argentina v. Uruguay)*, Judgment, ICJ Reports 2010.

*R. v. Taylor* (1928) 21 cr. App R 20.

*Rachel S. Grynberg, Stephen M. Grynberg, Miriam Z. Grynberg, and RSM Production Corp. v. Grenada*, ICSID Case No. ARB/10/6, Award dated Dec. 10, 2010.

*Re H (Minors)* [1996] AC 563.

*Rompetrol Group N.V. v. Romania*, ICSID Case No. ARB/06/3, Award dated May 6, 2013.

Rosenthal, John Terrence A. and Alter, Robert T., "Clear and Convincing to Whom? The False Claims Act And Its Burden of Proof Standard: Why the Government Needs a Big Stick," 75 NOTRE DAME L. REV. 1409 (2000).

Ross, Alison, "Fortier takes lead in development bank's corruption battle," Global Arbitration Review dated Sept. 20, 2016, available at https://globalarbitrationreview.com/article/1068603/fortier-takes-lead-in-development-bank%E2%80%99s-corruption-battle (last accessed Apr. 15, 2019).

*RSM Production Corp. v. Grenada*, ICSID Case No. ARB/05/14, Award dated Mar. 13, 2009.

*Rumeli Telekom A.S. and Telsim Mobil Telekomunikasyon Hizmetleir A.S. v. Republic of Kazakhstan*, ICSID Case No. ARB/05/16, Award dated July 29, 2008.

*Saipem S.p.A. v. The People's Republic of Bangladesh*, ICSID Case No. ARB/05/7, Award dated June 30, 2009.

Sandifer, Durward V., EVIDENCE BEFORE INTERNATIONAL TRIBUNALS (1975).

*SAUR International S.A. v. Republic of Argentina*, ICSID Case No. ARB/04/4, Decision on Jurisdiction and Liability dated June 6, 2012.

Schweizer, Mark, "The Civil Standard of Proof—What Is It, Actually?" *Max Planck Institute for Research on Collective Goods* (2013).

*Secretary of State for the Home Department v. Rehman (AP)* [2001] UKHL 47.

*Securities & Exchange Commission v. VimpelCom Ltd.*, Civil Case No. 16-cv-1266-VM, S.D.N.Y., Final Judgment dated Feb. 22, 2016.

South African Development Community Protocol against Corruption, adopted Aug. 14, 2001, entered into force Aug. 6, 2003.

*State v. Butler*, 94 N.E. 457 (1949).

Stiglitz, Joseph E. and Pieth, Mark, *Overcoming the Shadow Economy*, Friedrich Ebert Stiftung (Nov. 2016).

Stockholm District Court, Section 4, Goal no. B 12201-17, B 12203-17, Judgment dated Feb. 15, 2019.

*Sufficiency of Circumstantial Evidence in a Criminal Case*, 55 COL. L. REV. 549 (1955).

Swiss Federal Criminal Court, R.R.2013.205 + R.R.2013.206, Decision dated Nov. 5, 2013.

Swiss Federal Criminal Court, SK.2014.24, Decision dated Oct. 1, 2014 against Riadh Ben Aïssa.

Tapper and Colin, CROSS AND TAPPER ON EVIDENCE 121 (12th ed. 2010).

The OECD Convention on Bribery: A Commentary, edited by Mark Pieth, et al, 2nd ed., 2014.

*The Republic of Croatia v. MOL Hungarian Oil and Gas PLC*, PCA Case No. 2014–15, UNCITRAL, Final Award dated Dec. 23, 2016.

*Tokios Tokelės v. Ukraine*, ICSID Case No. ARB/02/18, Award dated July 26, 2007.

Tomka, Peter and Proulx, Vincent-Joel, *The Evidentiary Practice of the World Court*, National University of Singapore, Working Paper 2015/010, Dec. 2015.

*Tradex Hellas S.A. v. Republic of Albania*, ICSID Case No. ARB/94/2, Award dated Apr. 29, 1999.

Transparency International, Corruption Perceptions Index 2017 dated Feb. 21, 2018, available at https://www.transparency.org/news/feature/corruption_perceptions_index_2017 (last accessed Apr. 15, 2019).

Transparency International, Global Corruption Barometer dated Nov. 14, 2017, available at https://www.transparency.org/news/feature/global_corruption_barometer_citizens_voices_from_around_the_world (last accessed Apr. 15, 2019).

*Tza Yap Shum v. Republic of Peru*, ICSID Case No ARB/07/6, Award dated July 7, 2011.

U.N. Security Council 8346th Meeting, SC/13493 dated Sept. 10, 2018, "Global Cost of Corruption at Least 5 Per Cent of World Gross Domestic Product, Secretary-General Tells Security Council, Citing World Economic Forum Data," available at https://www.un.org/press/en/2018/sc13493.doc.htm (last accessed Apr. 25, 2019).

U.S. Department of Justice Office of Public Affairs, "Former Siemens Executive Pleads Guilty to Role in $100 Million Foreign Bribery Scheme," Mar. 15, 2018.

U.S. Securities and Exchange Commission, "SEC Charges Siemens AG for Engaging in Worldwide Bribery," Dec. 15, 2008.

*U.S. v. VimpelCom and Unitel*, Deferred Prosecution Agreement dated Feb. 22, 2016.

UNCITRAL Arbitration Rules (2013).

UNCITRAL Model Law on International Commercial Arbitration (1985, amended in 2006).

UNCITRAL Notes on Organizing Arbitral Proceedings.

*Unglaube v. Republic of Costa Rica*, ICSID Case No. ARB/08/1, Award dated May 16, 2012.

*Union Fenosa Gas, S.A. v. Arab Republic of Egypt*, ICSID Case No. ARB/14/4, Award dated Aug. 31, 2018.

*United Kingdom of Great Britain and Northern Ireland v. Albania* (*Corfu Channel*), ICJ, Judgment dated Apr. 9, 1949.

United Nations Convention Against Corruption, Resolution 58/4, adopted Oct. 31, 2003 by the UN General Assembly, entered into force Dec. 14, 2005.

United Nations Convention against Transnational Organized Crime and the Protocols Thereto, Resolution 55/25, adopted Nov. 15, 2000, entered into force Sept. 29, 2003.

United Nations Handbook on Practical Anti-Corruption Measures for Prosecutors and Investigators (Sept. 2004).

*United States of America v. Karimova*, Criminal Case No. 19-cr-00165-KMW, S.D.N.Y., Indictment dated Mar. 7, 2019.

*United States of America v. Mobile TeleSystems PJSC*, Criminal Case No. 19-cr-00167-JPO, S.D.N.Y., Criminal Information dated Mar. 6, 2019.

*United States of America v. Siemens S.A.* (*Argentina*), District Court for the District of Columbia, Criminal Case No. 08-368-RJL, Statement of Offense dated Dec. 15, 2008.

*United States of America v. Telia Company AB*, Criminal Case No. 1:17-cr-00581-GBD, S.D.N.Y., Criminal Information dated Sept. 21, 2017, Deferred Prosecution Agreement dated Sept. 21, 2017.

*United States of America v. Unitel*, Criminal Case No. 16-cr-137-ER, S.D.N.Y. Criminal Judgment dated Feb. 26, 2016.

*United States of America v. VimpelCom Ltd. and Unitel*, Criminal Case No. 16-cr-137-ER, S.D.N.Y., Court Transcript dated Feb. 18, 2016.

*United States of America v. VimpelCom Ltd. and Unitel*, Criminal Case No. 16-cr-137-ER, S.D.N.Y., Agreement dated Feb. 22, 2016.

*United States of America v. VimpelCom Ltd. and Unitel*, Criminal Case No. 16-cr-137-ER, S.D.N.Y., Deferred Prosecution Agreement dated Feb. 22, 2016.

United States Sentencing Commission, Guidelines Manual dated Nov. 1, 2015.

*United States v. Johns*, 26 Fed Cas. 616 No. 15481, C.C. Pa. 1806.

*United States v. Siemens Aktiengesellschaft*, District Court for the District of Columbia, Criminal Case No. CR-08-367-RJL, Plea Agreement Letter dated Dec. 15, 2008.

van Houtte, Vera, "Adverse Inferences in International Arbitration," *in* WRITTEN EVIDENCE AND DISCOVERY IN INTERNATIONAL ARBITRATION: NEW ISSUES AND TENDENCIES, Teresa Giovannini and Alexis Mourre (eds) dated 2009.

*Vladislav Kim and others v. Republic of Uzbekistan*, ICSID Case No. ARB/13/6, Decision on Jurisdiction dated Mar. 8, 2017.

von Wobeser, Claus, "The Corruption Defense and Preserving the Rule of Law," *in* INTERNATIONAL ARBITRATION AND THE RULE OF LAW: CONTRIBUTION AND CONFORMITY COMMENTARY 2017.

*Waguih George Siag and Clorinda Vecchi v. The Arab Republic of Egypt*, ICSID Case No. ARB/05/15, Award dated June 1, 2009.

*Waste Management v. Mexico*, ICSID Case No. ARB(AF)/00/3, Procedural Order Concerning Disclosure of Documents dated Oct. 1, 2002.

*Wena Hotels Ltd. v. Arab Republic of Egypt*, ICSID Case No. ARB/98/4, Award dated Dec. 8, 2000.

Williams, C.R., "Burdens and Standards in Civil Litigation," 25 SYDNEY L. REV. 165 (2003).

Woolf Committee, "Business Ethics, Global Companies and the Defence Industry" (May 2008).

*World Duty Free Co. Ltd. v. The Republic of Kenya*, ICSID Case No. ARB/00/7, Award dated Oct. 4, 2006.

*Yukos Universal Limited (Isle of Man) v. The Russian Federation*, PCA Case No. AA 227, Final Award dated July 18, 2014.

Ziadé, Nassib G., "Accountability for Corruption in Investment Arbitration: Equitable Remedies for Findings of Illegality," *in* BCDR INTERNATIONAL ARBITRATION REVIEW, Kluwer Law International 2016, Volume 3, Issue 2, Nassib G. Ziadé (ed).

www.ingramcontent.com/pod-product-compliance
Lightning Source LLC
Chambersburg PA
CBHW031330230926
51848CB00001B/172
*9789004369771*